Praise for *Inside the Minds*

"Need-to-read inside information and analysis that will improve your bottom line - the best source in the business." – Daniel J. Moore, Member, Harris Beach LLP

"The Inside the Minds series is a valuable probe into the thought, perspectives, and techniques of accomplished professionals…" – Chuck Birenbaum, Partner, Thelen Reid & Priest

"Aspatore has tapped into a gold mine of knowledge and expertise ignored by other publishing houses." – Jack Barsky, Managing Director, Information Technology & Chief Information Officer, ConEdison *Solutions*

"Unlike any other publisher – actual authors that are on the front-lines of what is happening in industry." – Paul A. Sellers, Executive Director, National Sales, Fleet and Remarketing, Hyundai Motor America

"A snapshot of everything you need…" – Charles Koob, Co-Head of Litigation Department, Simpson Thacher & Bartlet

"Everything good books should be - honest, informative, inspiring, and incredibly well-written." – Patti D. Hill, President, BlabberMouth PR

"Great information for both novices and experts." – Patrick Ennis, Partner, ARCH Venture Partners

"A rare peek behind the curtains and into the minds of the industry's best." – Brandon Baum, Partner, Cooley Godward

"Intensely personal, practical advice from seasoned dealmakers." – Mary Ann Jorgenson, Coordinator of Business Practice Area, Squire, Sanders & Dempsey

"Great practical advice and thoughtful insights." – Mark Gruhin, Partner, Schmeltzer, Aptaker & Shepard PC

"Reading about real-world strategies from real working people beats the typical business book hands down." – Andrew Ceccon, Chief Marketing Officer, OnlineBenefits Inc.

"Books of this publisher are syntheses of actual experiences of real-life, hands-on, front-line leaders--no academic or theoretical nonsense here. Comprehensive, tightly organized, yet nonetheless motivational!" – Lac V. Tran, Sr. Vice President, CIO and Associate Dean Rush University Medical Center

"Aspatore is unlike other publishers…books feature cutting-edge information provided by top executives working on the front-line of an industry." – Debra Reisenthel, President and CEO, Novasys Medical Inc.

www.Aspatore.com

Aspatore Books, a Thomson business, is the largest and most exclusive publisher of C-level executives (CEO, CFO, CTO, CMO, partner) from the world's most respected companies and law firms. Aspatore annually publishes a select group of C-level executives from the Global 1,000, top 250 law firms (partners and chairs), and other leading companies of all sizes. C-Level Business Intelligence™, as conceptualized and developed by Aspatore Books, provides professionals of all levels with proven business intelligence from industry insiders—direct and unfiltered insight from those who know it best—as opposed to third-party accounts offered by unknown authors and analysts. Aspatore Books is committed to publishing an innovative line of business and legal books, those which lay forth principles and offer insights that, when employed, can have a direct financial impact on the reader's business objectives, whatever they may be. In essence, Aspatore publishes critical tools—need-to-read as opposed to nice-to-read books—for all business professionals.

Inside the Minds

The critically acclaimed *Inside the Minds* series provides readers of all levels with proven business intelligence from C-level executives (CEO, CFO, CTO, CMO, partner) from the world's most respected companies. Each chapter is comparable to a white paper or essay and is a future-oriented look at where an industry/profession/topic is heading and the most important issues for future success. Each author has been carefully chosen through an exhaustive selection process by the *Inside the Minds* editorial board to write a chapter for this book. *Inside the Minds* was conceived in order to give readers actual insights into the leading minds of business executives worldwide. Because so few books or other publications are actually written by executives in industry, *Inside the Minds* presents an unprecedented look at various industries and professions never before available.

INSIDE THE MINDS

The Changing Role of Law Firm Librarianship
Leading Librarians on Developing Budgets, Evaluating Resources, and Responding to the Expanding Role of the Law Firm Library

Mat # 40729085

BOOK & ARTICLE IDEA SUBMISSIONS

If you are a C-Level executive, senior lawyer, or venture capitalist interested in submitting a book or article idea to the Aspatore editorial board for review, please email TLR.AspatoreAuthors@thomson.com. Aspatore is especially looking for highly specific ideas that would have a direct financial impact on behalf of a reader. Completed publications can range from 2 to 2,000 pages. Include your book/article idea, biography, and any additional pertinent information.

©2008 Thomson/Aspatore
All rights reserved. Printed in the United States of America.

Inside the Minds Project Manager, Merissa Kraham; edited by Michaela Falls; proofread by Melanie Zimmerman

No part of this publication may be reproduced or distributed in any form or by any means, or stored in a database or retrieval system, except as permitted under Sections 107 or 108 of the U.S. Copyright Act, without prior written permission of the publisher. This book is printed on acid free paper.

Material in this book is for educational purposes only. This book is sold with the understanding that neither any of the authors or the publisher is engaged in rendering legal, accounting, investment, or any other professional service. Neither the publisher nor the authors assume any liability for any errors or omissions or for how this book or its contents are used or interpreted or for any consequences resulting directly or indirectly from the use of this book. For legal advice or any other, please consult your personal lawyer or the appropriate professional.

The views expressed by the individuals in this book (or the individuals on the cover) do not necessarily reflect the views shared by the companies they are employed by (or the companies mentioned in this book) or Thomson Reuters. The employment status and affiliations of authors with the companies referenced are subject to change.

Aspatore books may be purchased for educational, business, or sales promotional use. For information, please email West.customer.service@thomson.com.

ISBN 978-0-314-98989-5

For corrections, updates, comments or any other inquiries please email TLR.AspatoreEditorial@thomson.com.

First Printing, 2008
10 9 8 7 6 5 4 3 2 1

Contents

D. Lynn Fogle   7
Manager of Library Services,
Greenebaum Doll & McDonald PLLC
CHANGE IS CONSTANT – MEET IT WITH A POSITIVE, COLLABORATIVE ATTITUDE

Mindy Maddrey   23
National Library Manager,
Sonnenschein Nath & Rosenthal
EVOLUTION OF LAW FIRM LIBRARIES AND LIBRARIANS: ONE DECADE OF PERSPECTIVE

Anne Stemlar   39
Director of Research and Library Services,
Goodwin Procter LLP
PROVIDING VALUE IN THE LEGAL INDUSTRY TODAY

Monice M. Kaczorowski   51
Director of Library Services, Neal, Gerber & Eisenberg LLP
THE PROACTIVE LAW LIBRARIAN

Mary Kay Jung   65
Director of Library Services, Thompson Coburn LLP
KEY ELEMENTS IN THE LAW FIRM LIBRARIAN'S CHANGING ROLE

Linda Will   73
Director of Information Services, Dorsey & Whitney
LIBRARIANSHIP: A PROFESSION IN TRANSITION

Laurie Daley   87
Librarian, **Bullivant Houser Bailey**
ACTIVE LIBRARIANSHIP IN THE
BUSINESS-ORIENTED LAW FIRM

Elaine M. Egan   97
Legal Information Manager, **Mayer Brown LLP**
LAW FIRM LIBRARIANSHIP: MOVING
TOWARD HARNESSING KNOWLEDGE IN A
CHANGING INFORMATIONAL LANDSCAPE

Lynn Connor Merring   109
Manager, Library, Records, and Docket,
Stradling Yocca Carlson & Rauth
THE LAW FIRM LIBRARIAN AND THE
BUSINESS OF LAW

Cindy Adams   117
Associate Director of Library Services,
McKenna Long & Aldridge LLP
LAW LIBRARIANSHIP, THEN AND NOW

Change is Constant – Meet it with a Positive, Collaborative Attitude

D. Lynn Fogle
Manager of Library Services
Greenebaum Doll & McDonald PLLC

Introduction

After a few years in public and academic libraries, I began working as a law firm librarian in 1985. The job advertisement I answered was one simple line—"law firm needs librarian with knowledge of computers," and being the new owner of a red-hot Apple IIc, I applied. I often think of that advertisement and how, in its brief and direct way, it captured the essence of my job for a very long time. It also reflected my firm's recognition of the changes in technology that were about to occur and their desire to adopt to those changes.

In the mid-eighties, law libraries and legal research were almost entirely print-based. Lexis and Westlaw were very new, evolving products. Each had recent case law files, but not much more to offer. Researchers of today would be shocked at the sparse content of those early systems. Search functionality was very crude. For the most part, case law research meant the West digests or the ALR annotation system. Case verification meant using a stack of Shepards Citations. There were no computer networks, no Internet, no list-servs, no blogs. E-mail and CD-ROM technology were still on the horizon.

In a paper-based world, the library maintenance was essentially clerical. Routing, filing, and shelving were daily, time-consuming chores. There was no automated case printing or cutting and pasting; cases were physically photocopied stacks at a time. During major litigation projects, 40 percent of the state case reporters could be off the shelf.

Many law firm libraries were run by efficient para-professionals—bright people who were in the right place at the right time. Staffing ratios were around two to three clerical people for each MLS librarian. By the year 2000, this ratio had flipped the other way. Today, the clerical maintenance of our collection is a very small portion of the library workload, as our collections are now in a variety of formats. Our staffs are more technically skilled. Old jobs have been eliminated and replaced with more technically skilled ones. We now spend as much time maintaining Web sites and digital collections as we do print with librarians who support Microsoft Sharepoint and SQL databases.

CHANGE IS CONSTANT – MEET IT WITH A POSITIVE, COLLABORATIVE ATTITUDE

Why is the role of the librarian changing today? Technology. And technology has changed the library in more areas than just the format of information. It's more than just moving the printed text from paper to a computer screen; these changes affected the way people thought of information and really changed the way they acquired and used it. The digitization of the information released it from many boundaries and limitations endemic to paper. Digitization has allowed us to slice and dice information, to deliver and find it in ways that were previously unimagined.

We moved from weekly printed newsletters to e-mailed versions, which our attorneys welcomed. E-mail eliminated the wait for the paper copy. Everyone got information quickly and that immediacy became the standard. Now we have blogs and news aggregators pulling topical news and information and delivering it to users via e-mail, RSS feeds, and object-based reporting populating our portal pages. Sometimes it feels as if we moved from a two-dimensional information world to a three-dimensional world in a short span of time.

As the business and legal world became more sophisticated, the administrative part of the large firm law practice also expanded with more executive non-lawyer specialists. The complexity of information management changed the librarian's role within the law firm tremendously, leading us to areas of collaboration with IT, records management, marketing, litigation support, and knowledge management. It is very important to understand each of the areas and to develop good working relationships with each group. As data is increasingly stored electronically, it becomes a part of records management, data management, and knowledge management.

A common phenomenon in law firms is if you do one job well, you'll be asked to do other jobs well. Several times during my tenure with my firm, I've been asked to step in as an office manager, which I am glad to do as long as it is for a few months, not years. I can't emphasize enough what an eye-opening experience this was. For instance, I had access to a lot of information about the firm management that I didn't have before. This gave me a tremendously different perspective. I've also had to supervise records but gladly surrendered it to someone with greater expertise. All of these experiences gave me valuable insight into the ways different areas of the firm operate which, in turn, really helps me partner with those groups.

A successful law firm librarian needs to be a strategic manager who is able to collaborate with various units of the firm while working toward the common goals of the firm. You will not be successful without the support of the top-level management or the peer level managers of your organization. Not everyone will have the opportunity to be a temporary office manager or records manager, but you can learn a lot about those areas by befriending your peer managers and doing a little current awareness reading on the legal industry. Don't feel isolated and don't work isolated.

The Changes and the Response

I think that librarians have generally embraced new technologies and new research tools, but it has not been an easy transition—perhaps an easier change for some than others. Whenever I think of this, I am instantly reminded of a story that Bob Berring told frequently at law library meetings in the 1990s regarding change. With apologies to Mr. Berring, the story went something like this.

Being of the generation that grew up with the western as a very popular movie genre, Mr. Berring compared the "cattle drive" to our journey of technology change for both librarians and library users. A cattle drive involved the cowboys walking the steers many miles over sometimes difficult and dangerous terrain to market. The herd would eventually come to a river to be crossed. A few adventurous steers would jump into the water and forge the stream. Then, with pressure from the cowboys, the majority of the herd would enter the river and slowly make their way across. Lastly, there would be a few stragglers that were forced into the water and maybe a few who tangled themselves in brush and were left behind.

A humorous but accurate analogy of how people move with change and technology in all areas of librarianship. Most people move with the herd when they have to; those who don't move will get left behind. With law firms in particular, adapting to new methods has been critical; new technology has driven and expanded the already multi-faceted role of the librarian.

CHANGE IS CONSTANT – MEET IT WITH A POSITIVE, COLLABORATIVE ATTITUDE

Here, librarians have to keep pace with their users in both technology and research methods—and that is very difficult to do, as the rate of development with technology is only increasing. To paraphrase Darwin, it is not the strongest who survive, it is the most adaptable. In order to adapt successfully, it is crucial to have cooperative working relationships with other managers of the firm so that it is possible to cope with changes together. It is immensely helpful if you can cross-train each other, budget together, and work toward a common goal.

Librarians are finders, filterers, and creators of information, but perhaps our primary area is research. It's been very interesting to see the research tools and methods evolve. Research has moved from printed indexes to the brave new world of full-text searching. Recently we saw the merger of those traditional and new search methods. Publishers are beginning to incorporate the best features of both print and online by pulling together traditional print tools, such as tables of content, subject indexes, and lists of cases into the online version, making a better product.

This evolution in research has made training a high priority for most law firm librarians as we strive for research competency for our legal staff. Our library staff has provided a variety of training opportunities for a long time, but three years ago, we developed a more structured training program, one that coordinates specialized training from vendors and offers a variety of in-house training. One of our senior librarians is the coordinator. Every year we offer a short series of classes for our summer and fall associates, which covers basic skills and information to ease them from an academic to firm research environment. We also target specific practice areas each year; for example, one year we concentrated on offering several classes for the tax group. Some of our training efforts are not traditional classes. We have had success in taking five-minute training capsules into the attorneys' offices. Part of our training process includes needs assessment and the compilation of statistics that we distribute to our management.

One rule we emphasize in training with all of our attorneys—and this is our mantra as well—you must constantly evaluate your research methods and information sources. You must always be willing to learn new ways of finding information because the methods and resources constantly change.

Wireless technologies, data management, and resource sharing technologies are changing at an extraordinary pace. All of our legal staff and management have firm BlackBerries. Many of our users have wireless laptops and regularly do writing and research from many locations using a VPN. This gives us challenges and opportunities in the way we deliver information. The BlackBerry has affected users' ability to receive current awareness material in a very positive way. It is also very common for attorneys to send quick reference questions via their BlackBerry and expect a fast answer back. This expectation of quick reference turnaround has led us to change the way we receive reference questions. Most of these come via e-mail to library groups where the first available librarian will pick up the question and deliver the response. This has been very effective in coping with reference demands covering multiple offices. A virtual private network (VPN) is a private, secured Web connection to our firm network that lets the user work online exactly as they would in the office. Unfortunately, though, transparent authentication to our Web subscriptions does not work, because those are set up using the firm's IP addresses so solutions to these problems must be devised as they crop up.

Other areas of interest are the law firm industry's methods for data management, including records and document management systems that are really related knowledge management issues. The need for data storage and management is growing tremendously and affects all law firm data managers. For example, we have a new knowledge management project of imaging and indexing a very large amount of administrative documents for a practice group. After consulting with our IT director and records manager, we agreed that the best plan would be to image the documents and profile them into the document management system (DMS). They are profiled using firm records management standards, which will affect our ability to manipulate them in the future. Finally, they'll be pulled into West KM from the DMS where they will be full text searchable from our portal and Westlaw. Having them saved and profiled in this way made everyone happy. We devised the project and procedures pretty quickly because the key departments collaborated. Each person had their own piece of the puzzle or recommendation and it was a win-win for the firm.

We have been involved in intranet and portal development for ten years and we currently have a specialized law portal that uses Sharepoint as a base. We

Change is Constant – Meet it with a Positive, Collaborative Attitude

are very interested in what Microsoft is doing with Sharepoint as, with every new release, it becomes an increasingly important part of the Microsoft platform. Again, this has been a collaborative project with IT, in which IT handles most of the technical issues, and the library handles policy issues, content population, and development. It has been a great team effort.

One of the most difficult issues for a legal librarian today tends to be those dealing with licensing agreements and copyrights. Converting to electronic information has simplified the distribution of information and eliminated some of the copyright problems associated with print; however, license agreements tend to have new problems and restrictions and should be scrutinized. It is important to read and understand the contents of these agreements. Many librarians find proposed licensing agreements to be overly restrictive, but lack the skills to negotiate the terms beneficial to the firm. One rule of thumb, don't be afraid to ask for what you want; they can only say no and they might say yes. Also, don't be afraid to consult with the firm's management or commercial lawyers for negotiation advice. As this is a common problem for law librarians, it has become a popular topic of continuing education programs.

Marketing the Law Library

In order to promote the services of a firm's library, law librarians generally make use of internal marketing techniques such as brochures, internal Web pages, staff lunch-and-learns, branding, and emphasizing "best practices" among others. We have printed brochures on our librarians and services that we distribute to new users and at training sessions. We brand all our handouts and replicate this branding, materials, and information on our internal Web pages. Remember, you have professional marketers as business partners in the firm. They can give you great advice and resources. We have found that our marketing department is very valuable in helping us develop our competitive intelligence research. It's a perfect team project. They frequently receive or initiate the project, the library does the substantive research, and they repackage the information and deliver it.

We find getting before a captive audience, such as a practice group meeting, very helpful in reminding folks of our skills and resources. Essentially, though, effective marketing boils down to visibility and good service. You have to make sure to keep reminding folks of library services. It is difficult in today's world to attract and maintain someone's attention. Once you do get their attention, though, you have to live up to expectations and provide excellent service. If you fail in providing good service, you won't get their attention again.

In the "post-Google" landscape, everyone is a researcher. I have noticed something that I call "The First Warm Body" method of research, wherein the attorney asks the first warm body they encounter in the hallway to find information. Of course, that person is usually a secretary, paralegal, or attorney. The library finds out about the question when the First Warm Body fails to find the answer, and the researcher has to turn to the library staff for help. In the instances when the question never reaches the proper library staff, one has to wonder, did the First Warm Body give an adequate answer?

In general, however, attorneys value sophisticated research in legal issues, public records, marketing, and general business areas. They are still impressed with the so-called "rabbit out of the hat" research, finding the impossible fact or figure. They remember that sort of thing. They also like training and assistance with current awareness filtering and coping with some of the new information technologies. Sometimes it is not just a training issue, but rather an explanation of how and why the new technology works this way. They don't need to just learn the new method; they need to understand the evolution. The "why" can be as important as the "how."

Challenges Facing the Law Firm Librarian—Financial Considerations

As mentioned previously, keeping up with technology changes in law practice and research, including all the Web-based sources for information, is by far the greatest challenge facing today's law firm librarians. Keeping up with the management and business side is important, too.
A key challenge for librarians in management positions is fiscal responsibility—an important, but sometimes difficult task. Print and electronic subscriptions remain expensive, and new opportunities in areas such as knowledge management, portals, and CI come with a high price tag. It is important to manage those costs, understand them, and understand how the firm management views them in the greater scheme of things.

Change is Constant – Meet it with a Positive, Collaborative Attitude

I work closely with my executive director. He gives me areas that need to be watched, as well as advice on how the firm views and compares this information. I also work closely with our accounting department and can ask them spending and statistical information. Some areas I would recommend librarians monitor besides overall gross spending would be library costs per attorney ratio, Lexis/Westlaw costs per attorney ratio, and what percent is library spending of the total budget. Monitoring those ratios over time is very important. Bottom-line costs may increase and costs per attorney may increase, but budget ratio of library spending may stay the same. For example, our costs increase approximately 5 to 10 percent each year which means my bottom-line spending would be graphed on a steady increase. However, if I graphed the library spending/firm budget ratio, it would be pretty flat because that ratio has been between 4 and 6 percent for twenty years. This means your costs are only growing proportionally with other firm costs. Your slice of the budget pie has not grown; it has stayed the same. These ratios also give you a good figure to use for benchmarking with other firms and with national averages. These sorts of statistics are usually available from professional organizations such as ALA or consulting groups like Hildebrandt.

Print costs continue rising, with electronic subscription costs rising at an even faster rate. Many of those costs are unique, and it is difficult to negotiate a competitive price. There has also been a recent change in the area of cost recovery. A few firms no longer charge Lexis and Westlaw back to clients—it is considered overhead. A few firms still charge back everything, but for the most part, many clients negotiate the online fees out of their engagement letter. So, many firms still have a policy of charging back, but in reality only part of their clients pay for online charges. It will be interesting to see how this plays out, but I predict that more firms will stop charging back altogether.

Our budget is much larger than it was, say, two or three years ago. Some of that is caused by cost increases of existing material and subscriptions, as I mentioned; however, some of the large increases are new categories. We eliminated some general ledger codes in print areas and created new ones to track new projects. We also share some expenses with other departments such as IT and marketing. For example, some of our KM expenses might be split between the library and IT while some of it might be under a code that we share.

In terms of new products, several people are asked to evaluate a product, whether it is a new Web subscription, software, e-mail, etc. Key factors that we look at include ease of use, size, and quality of content and, of course, cost. Comparisons are then made with comparable products to determine the best solution at the best cost. Again, collaboration is the key to success. If most of the parties agree, the product or project will have "buy-in" from those people and everyone will work to make it successful.

Benchmarking Success for the Library

I used to think benchmarking was a very exact science and that each year I needed to buy special library or law firm industry benchmarking information. But over the years, I've developed a more serendipitous way to benchmark. There are certain financial ratios I monitor closely which I discussed previously. There is also casual benchmarking that I monitor via contact with other firm librarians, whether it is done in person, professional reading, continuing education, etc. If you keep up with law firm library activities in your current reading, you'll have a good idea where you fall on the benchmarking scale.

I also find a checklist to be a useful benchmarking tool for good library service:

--Are the librarians and attorneys able to answer research questions appropriately? If not, is this a staff training issue, or lack of necessary resources?
--Are the attorneys able to locate resources both in print and online, internally and externally?
--Is the library involved in information and knowledge initiatives in the firm? If not, ask to be included.
--Do other administrative groups (HR, marketing, IT, records) ask for your participation? If not, make sure they know what you can offer them.
--Do you interact with the firm's management on a regular basis? Are you able to answer their questions?

--What about library services in other firms? Do you feel your services are the same or are you being left behind? Talk with them. Share ideas.

Again, the law librarian's primary goal and objective is to provide excellent quality service to the attorneys so that they can meet the needs of our clients. The areas concentrated on are research competency, collection balancing, knowledge sharing, and management. The amount of time necessary to spend on each specific area is shaped by industry trends and organizational needs.

Part of providing excellent service is using information from professional education and current awareness to convey new ideas to the firm, rather than waiting to have the firm approach us first. This information exchange is a two-way street, but I do not want my executive director learning about law library trends and initiatives from his professional education. I want to tell him about it before he attends ALA.

Keeping up to date with information and the presentation of information technology techniques is always an organizational challenge. At times librarians struggle just to get a seat at the table and have a hard time being heard. Sometimes they have a voice but cannot always get necessary budgeting.

Training for New Librarians

The jurisdiction of librarians within law firms has expanded in recent years, especially in the areas of CI, recruiting, and knowledge management. This is a natural evolution considering that librarians are information specialists. The first areas to change were records and conflicts. Knowledge management and CI followed. In light of these recent changes, there are some key issues to consider in the training of the new generation of librarians.

Most current managers have one basic management class in library school and not much else. Most of us learned about management as we went along or from continuing education classes. The trend I currently see in law firm librarianship is an increasing number of specialists—portal specialists, CI specialists, and others—and I wonder if it will be harder for them to move out of the specialties into management roles. I believe our professional associations are aware of these career needs and are working to provide helpful education programs.

Additional Skills

To be successful in a law firm environment it is important to have very good communication and relationship building skills. It is always important to be able to express yourself clearly, but a law firm is a relatively small community compared to public libraries, and nearly everyone is well educated, has good writing and verbal skills, and they expect the same from everyone around them. If you struggle to explain yourself or a project in a competent manner, you are likely to be discounted altogether.

Positive relationship building is one of the most important elements of our work. It provides the core for our ability to work together as a team. You have to build positive relationships with the library team, patrons, peer managers, administration, business partners, and professional colleagues in other organizations. If you support the people around you, they will no doubt return the favor, and everyone will concentrate on mutually working toward firm objectives.

Stephen Covey, in *Seven Habits of Highly Effective People*, explains the concept of building an emotional bank account with the people around you. Simply, if you show kindness, consideration, and helpfulness to others, you make positive deposits in your emotional bank account. Then, on a rough day when you aren't so charming, folks will cut you a break because this isn't representative of your normal behavior. You still have many positive deposits and you've only made a minor withdrawal. On the other hand, if you are self-centered, rude, and generally unpleasant, your emotional bank account is empty—you aren't going to get any favors from anyone.

Once I was doing an "elevator talk" with a former IT director with our firm, trying to advocate something or other. His response was, "I don't care what you think because you are not a voting member of the executive committee." What a deal killer! I continued to work with him, but I have to say it was difficult after his comment. I have forgotten what we were discussing, but I'll never forget that comment. This incident was the exception to the rule, which has generally been that most people are nice and cooperative if you're nice and cooperative with them.

I mentioned some of the standard ideas above regarding marketing and advertising library services firm wide, but I also want to specify the importance of communication with your direct superiors. It is very important that the executive director, or your immediate superior, never be caught off guard about the library activities. It is embarrassing to them not to have full information and to be caught unawares about the departments they supervise. It is very important to cultivate this line of communication.

Some additional key attributes include:

a. Attitude. You have to have the right attitude, which means being open-minded and willing to embrace new ideas. It does not mean that you should implement every new thing that comes along, but it does mean you need to be committed to educating yourself about new changes. If you are close minded, you will accomplish nothing. Be fearless—do not let your fears prevent you from learning more about your trade.

b. Manners. Work fairly, professionally, and collaboratively with others, both internally and externally. You need to build solid relationships with your patrons, your management, your co-workers, and your vendors. Building positive relationships with vendors is important because they are in fact your business partners. Some might call this networking, but it is more than just adding someone to your contacts—here you are building your core community.

c. Learn. Educate yourself. Read. Build your knowledge base. You can learn quite a bit from free sources on the Internet, from library professionals such as Nina Platt, Sabrina Pacifici, and Genie Tyburski. Go to a professional library meeting or do CE via webx. Library and law firm vendors frequently host free webx programs. This is an excellent way to keep up and learn about new things. Do not limit yourself to just library information, though. Subscribe to law.com's daily e-mail and other legal industry news sources. Read *American Lawyer*, *The Wall Street Journal*, and *Law Technology News*. You need to know the headlines pertinent to business and industry. And of course, you can always learn from your peers.

d. Accept new challenges and roles when the time is right. Convince the firm to pursue knowledge initiatives and let you work in new areas. Again, do not be afraid to try. It is always better to lead change than to be passive and vulnerable to the results.

e. Repeat the steps above. Change is an infinite cycle.

Additional Key Resources

Most of the library associations—AALL, SLA, and others—have provided programs that were helpful in managing the changing role of librarianship. I also find some of the vendor support groups, such as West and Lexis Librarian Relations, extremely helpful. In addition to functioning as company liaisons, they have provided extensive coaching and teaching on many areas of law firm management and law librarianship. Not only have these helped me build my skills, I have found them to be some of the best motivational programs available. A real career turning point for me was attending a Thomson University sponsored program on change in the 1990s. It had a profound impact on my attitude about my work and my own abilities.

The Web sites of the Law Library Resource Exchange (LLRX) and The Virtual Chase have been extraordinarily helpful during the last few years, and Nina Platt's new site, The Strategic Librarian, is also a wonderful resource.

I know that the Private Law Libraries (PLL) division of AALL has supported alliances with several other professional groups including the Association of Legal Administrators, the American Bar Association, and the Legal Marketing Association. I believe the relationship between AALL/PLL and ALA has been very successful.

Conclusion

The best piece of advice I can offer is to accept and embrace change as an integral part of your work and career, and to develop a positive, proactive attitude to deal with it. If you have these in order, the skill building and management skills will fall into place. Also, avoid thinking that taking on new roles is too hard for you because you are in a small city or in a mid-size or smaller firm, because the playing field is level in today's world. Just try. You may surprise yourself and rise to the occasion.

D. Lynn Fogle is the manager of library services for the law firm of Greenebaum Doll & McDonald PLLC, where she supervises library services for six offices, manages knowledge management projects, collaborates on the firm portal, and does extensive Internet research. Ms. Fogle received her B.A. degree from Transylvania University and her M.L.S. degree from the University of Kentucky. She has spoken at continuing education seminars for attorneys, paralegals, and librarians on subjects relating to technology and the Internet. She is a member of the American Association of Law Libraries, Special Library Association, and the Southeastern Association of Law Libraries.

Dedication: *To my parents, who taught me to learn as much as I could.*

Evolution of Law Firm Libraries and Librarians: One Decade of Perspective

Mindy Maddrey

National Library Manager

Sonnenschein Nath & Rosenthal

The History of Law Firm Librarianship

Initially, law librarians functioned as more or less traditional librarians, managing vast quantities of print material. We worked with a large number of specialized legal publishers to obtain a great variety of highly specialized print materials, most of which were kept up to date through loose-leaf filing or separate volume supplements. We served a mixed audience of users, consisting almost entirely of partners, associates, and paralegals. A great deal of our time was spent developing and maintaining our collections, seeking out niche resources.

Most libraries were structured with formal divisions between reference services and technical services. A small percentage of librarians worked in the then-emerging field of "electronic services," focusing on providing vague equivalents to print resources via dial-up services, floppy disks, and/or CDs.

Correspondence with our patrons and with other librarians was largely conducted in person or by telephone. Associations, such as the national American Association of Law Libraries or the local Law Librarians Society of DC, provided vital means for librarians to meet like-minded people. Interlibrary loan, a backbone for locating challenging, narrowly focused material, was conducted by highly integrated individuals, who relied on direct contact with librarian friends and colleagues to meet their firms' needs.

Physical libraries were typically showpieces for firms, situated in central spaces, often with windows, art, and architectural features to maximize their attractiveness. The library functioned as a meeting place and a workspace; researchers commonly pulled hundreds of volumes from the shelves on a daily basis as attorneys and staff tracked down specific legal references. Associates regularly gathered to talk about their work and their personal lives.

Recent Trends

In the intervening years, however, advancing technology has changed every aspect of library science, as applied in a law firm library. For example, law firm libraries have seen a significant reduction of print materials, in favor of electronic equivalents. Print materials are increasingly expensive in terms of actual purchase cost, shipping and handling, physical space in pricy law firm real estate, and maintenance costs for loose-leaf filing. By contrast, electronic resources provide access to legal materials no matter where an attorney is located physically. As more and more attorneys work from home or travel on business, they find that they are freed from the need to travel to a physical library to complete their research.

While software programs have not settled on absolute standards, an increasing number of file formats have become standardized. Most users can open most files without worrying about specific program patches, further freeing them to rely on their home computers, their laptops, their BlackBerries, their cell phones, and the myriad of other electronic tethers surrounding most attorneys, paralegals, and staff.

Today, all librarians function as "electronic services" librarians. Technical services staff routinely manage integrated library system programs that are more sophisticated than the most advanced software used in any law firm department two decades ago. Reference services staff regularly access research services from major and minor vendors, relying on Internet connectivity and data transfer speeds that make our old modems seem like quaint museum pieces.

Firms increasingly rely on "portals," the current generation of intranets, harnessing the power of the World Wide Web for internal usage. Library staff members often become central players in portal development, serving as content providers and designers (given librarians' familiarity with dozens of research interfaces).

In addition, librarians find that more and more of their communications with patrons are conducted by electronic means. Most reference requests are received by phone or by e-mail (or by instant message, in a few forward-looking firms). Most responses are delivered by e-mail. Librarians no longer have the opportunity to chat with users around physical tables, over physical cups of coffee. Instead, we need to find new methods of building rapport with our patrons, including special training sessions, going to attorneys' scheduled practice group luncheons, and making concerted efforts to visit door to door (for those attorneys still working in the office on a regular basis).

Librarians' communication with fellow librarians has changed as well. We rely heavily on listservs (electronic mailing lists that distribute e-mails simultaneously to all subscribers) to ask questions of our colleagues, even to the extent of conducting virtually all inter-library loans through local and national listservs. In order to restore a sense of community, some librarians become more active with their local chapters of the American Association of Law Libraries, but there remains an overall loss in the sense of cohesive librarian communities.

The Changing Role of Librarianship

Legal Issues Related to Current Librarianship Duties

The most pressing legal issue relating to law librarianship is copyright (and its close cousin, contractual obligations regarding copying). Librarians are constantly being challenged to assess the fair use exception to copyright, balancing the nature and extent of material being copied, the effect on copyright holders' markets, and the for-profit nature of most law firm practice.

Copyright and contract issues are sharpened by an increasing reliance on electronic materials, particularly in the arena of interlibrary loan. While firms used to be able to lend a print copy of a book or a journal without creating any copy, now firms are often asked to forward electronic files, or to print resources from electronic holdings.

As law firms become more aggressive in marketing their services, copyright and contract issues multiply. Understandably, firms want to send clients copies of articles where attorneys are quoted, or where potential legal problems are analyzed. Law firms, in general, wrestle with acquiring appropriate legal clearance on these and other matters. Sometimes the library is asked to take the lead on these matters; other times, marketing or other administrative departments will spearhead the efforts. In all cases, the legal complexities abound.

Marketing Library Services

Librarians continue to face a substantial challenge in marketing their services to attorneys, paralegals, and staff throughout their firms. While librarians traditionally hosted get-togethers in the library (offering food and drink), hosted breakfasts and lunches (offering food and drink), or maintained a reference desk at the entrance to physical space (offering at least food, in the form of a candy bowl), many of those tried-and-true methods of getting attorney attention no longer work. In addition, most library patrons are overwhelmed by communications from people in their firms—they receive far too many e-mails on a daily basis. Moreover, attorneys and paralegals are expected to bill more hours than ever before to underwrite their very large and rapidly growing salaries; they do not have extra time to spend on anything that cannot be billed.

Marketing remains important, however. When a library successfully presents itself to its end users, it guarantees that it will get scarce budget funds during tight fiscal times. It secures a position of leadership in firm decisions, such as whether and how to implement a portal. Library managers who are recognized by their patrons as firm leaders are able to accomplish more, professionally and personally.

Some marketing efforts are successful. Libraries should strive to have a single, consistent image on all of their work product, promoting themselves through the quality of their work. Wherever possible, a uniform logo should be used, immediately alerting patrons to the source of the valuable information they are using. E-mail signature blocks, footers on word processing documents, cover sheets for printed materials—every document issuing from a library should acknowledge the library as the document source.

Librarians should strive to match their marketing messages to attorneys' needs. For example, rather than merely stating that the library can retrieve information about businesses, librarians should stress that the library has been instrumental in the successful completion of seven responses to requests for proposal in the past quarter. Alternatively, librarians can stress that the library can complete research at a cost-effective rate, providing greater value for firm clients. It is important to pitch marketing messages to attorneys' fiscal sensibilities, always focusing on how the library can most benefit the patron (rather than making vague appeals for patrons to visit the library.) It is also helpful to mask training sessions as continuing legal education and get certification for the library's training programs to lure more attorney patrons (in states where attorneys have mandatory CLE requirements).

In addition, librarians should choose targeted times of the year to invite users to specific events, giving attorneys, paralegals, and staff a chance to meet the people behind the e-mail messages. National Library Week and Banned Books Week are logical staging times, but any regular structured marketing campaign can be successful. Consider sending print invitations (created on color printers, where possible), given the relative rarity of print communications in many firms today. Remember that most users have substantial limitations on their time; do not expect anyone to linger more than fifteen minutes in the midst of a busy work day.

More than ever, libraries and librarians need to position themselves as solutions to problems (rather than consumers of firm resources).

Developing New Procedures and Practices

In an era of constant law firm mergers, it is vitally important for libraries to have written policies and procedures for all aspects of their practice. Such manuals provide training for new staff; reminders for existing staff; and demonstrate a clear blueprint for the merging of print, electronic, and human resources when libraries combine.

Our library, which serves 700 attorneys in fourteen offices, relies on a series of internal "Task Forces" to document policies and procedures. Staff is polled and volunteers are requested to assist with the development of a specific policy. Once a Task Force is identified, it meets multiple times, determining the policies currently in effect in each of our offices. It also surveys library peers at other firms (sometimes in person, sometimes through requests on national listservs), and it studies the literature of library management to determine best practices. After applying that knowledge, the Task Force then drafts written policies and procedures that are circulated to all staff for review and comment. After final revisions, the procedures become part of the library manual, which is posted on our internal portal page, accessible to all library staff, firm wide.

Jurisdiction of Librarians

Librarians' responsibility in many firms has changed substantially in recent years, both contracting and expanding. While a majority of library managers continue to report directly to their firm's executive director or chief operating officer, many libraries have been folded into information services or information technology departments. Many librarians find themselves reporting to Chief Information Officers. That contraction of responsibility and/or deepening of reporting hierarchy can result in perceived weakening of library status within firms.

At the same time, however, many librarians are charged with managing departments other than libraries. It is not uncommon for librarians to manage the records department, conflicts, and/or paralegal staff. Librarians are generally viewed as strong organizers of information; therefore, they are often given management roles in departments that handle physical papers, electronic files, and research.

The growth of implementation of knowledge management programs provides librarians with a possible area of expansion in firm hierarchies. Library managers are well suited for directing knowledge management programs, folding in many of their existing job responsibilities, particularly in the context of portals. While the title of Chief Knowledge Officer is not yet common, it provides an opportunity for forward-thinking library managers.

Managerial Training for Next Generation Law Firm Librarians

Most library managers have received little formal training for their positions. Most library schools offer a single course on management, focusing on a variety of relatively abstract theories about personnel management. Otherwise, most library managers "grow" into their positions, learning on the job from predecessors and working through a series of jobs with increasing responsibility.

Traditionally, library managers have needed to understand the nature of their resources, becoming extremely familiar with print and electronic research tools so that patrons' immediate needs are met. Managers have also needed to negotiate annual budgets, justifying purchases and explaining often exorbitant price increases. Annual reviews required managerial skill, as individual librarians were groomed for positions of increasing responsibility.

However, current library managers function as executives in sophisticated businesses. As law firms merge into entities of several hundred attorneys, they no longer act like small coalitions of friendly partners working toward a common goal. Law firm managers, including librarians, are forced to manage tremendously complicated enterprises with relatively gigantic budgets and complexities that were not imagined a decade ago.

Librarians need to use traditional business tools to manage entities of this size and complexity. One vital tool is a strategic plan—a concise statement of a library's goals, objectives, and tasks. Developing a strategic plan assists library management in multiple ways. A plan forces management to consider its priorities, to define precisely where problems exist and how those problems can be resolved. When a plan is presented to management, it educates the power structure of a firm about the value of the library. Once a plan has been approved and adopted by management, it provides a backbone for every decision—controversial or not—that is implemented within a library.

In addition, managing librarians must be able to discuss the library's functioning in traditional financial terms. Librarians not only need to structure a budget, they need to *understand* that budget. They need to know how to read spreadsheets, and they must be able to create spreadsheets that are clear. Excel and other spreadsheet programs have become a mandatory specialty for law firm library managers—formulas, summations, sorts, and subtotals should be second nature in the high stakes business world in which we now work. These technological tools can be harnessed to provide concrete illustrations, demonstrating how the firm has grown, how costs have increased, or how practice group membership has fluctuated. While the specific metrics will vary from firm to firm, the spreadsheet tools for demonstrating those measurements are uniform.

Finally, library managers must be able to make a business case, harnessing their strategic plan, as illustrated through fiscal analysis, to demonstrate to law firm management why specific resources are necessary. The specifics of a successful business case will vary from firm to firm, but each librarian should always ask, "How can I shape fulfillment of my needs into an advantage for my users?"

Financial Elements of Librarianship

Librarians have always been under pressure to save money; however, those pressures have reached epidemic proportions. In an era where unplanned associate raises may cost a law firm millions of dollars in any given year, library managers must be prepared to measure every penny in their budgets.

For years, many firms have enjoyed the luxury of duplicating print resources with electronic equivalents. While many—if not most—firms have stopped purchasing federal and state reporters in print, we often continue to buy treatises, statutes, and other materials in duplicate, paying for paper copies while we have electronic versions available.

That resource duplication becomes even more expensive as print publishers raise the cost of their offerings, often charging hefty fees for even minimal supplementation. Shipping and handling costs skyrocket, and staff costs for loose-leaf filing continue to rise.

All of these costs increase the pressure to switch to electronic resources. That switch creates a major challenge for law firm librarians, who must promote the new electronic equivalents, fully educating users regarding new online tools. Library staff must continue to generate teaching materials that are as effective at training the traditional print user as they are at training the new law school graduate who has never seen some resources in print (e.g., Shepard's Citator).

Librarians used to be able to assume that all their users were starting at the same level of technological awareness. We could structure training programs using carefully prepared scripts, knowing that each researcher likely had the same background. Today's training programs, though, need to take into account the fact that some attorneys have never conducted a simple search on Google. Other patrons, though, routinely use sophisticated Web applications, applying complicated syntax and strategies to identify specific information.

When training Luddites and technophiles, librarians must become creative. Sometimes, it is necessary to offer "remedial" classes, designed to bring all users up to a basic level of competence before anything of substance is taught. Other times it is necessary to structure two or more "tracks," so that advanced users are taught in an environment wholly separate from novice users. Increasingly, librarians should consider offering professional coaching, one-on-one training designed to address individuals' specific needs and abilities.

Evaluating Technologies

Often, librarians confront multiple tools that meet the same basic research needs, albeit with differing techniques or interfaces. For example, market intelligence can be obtained via West Monitor Suite or LexisNexis atVantage, with Bloomberg providing a strong alternative. Libraries are well served to evaluate these competitive products, in order to determine which best meet their needs.

The specific evaluation criteria vary by individual product. Users should structure a list of their requirements and expectations prior to beginning any comparative product review. Actual product usage can be compared to this master requirements list, to preserve fairness and to guarantee a thorough review.

Librarians should consider their own ability to use products, along with the abilities of their users. If a product is being considered for a practice group that consists entirely of users who have difficulty with technological tools, the library evaluator should select a product with a simple interface and clear instructions, even if some functionality is sacrificed. If, however, a tool is being selected for a highly sophisticated user pool, robustness of product (regardless of interface) might take priority.

For example, a novice user who needs access to regular opinions from the federal courts might be directed to Lexis's Daily Opinion Service. The technophobe can use that resource to receive updates on case law, limiting research results by working through a series of drop-down menus, without any knowledge of Boolean searching, alert technology, or other more sophisticated interface strategies. An experienced user, however, might want to exercise more control over his or her search, logging in to Lexis to structure a Boolean-based search, trading off ease of set-up for specificity of results.

In either case, the librarian's mission remains the same when guiding users toward appropriate resources: to put him or herself into the place of end users to determine the best solution.

Successfully Navigating the Changing Role of Librarianship

I believe that there are five main strategies for successfully navigating the changing role of librarianship:

1.) Keep in touch with your users and know your patrons—all of them. Take the time to learn and understand what all of your users do and how they fit into the firm. Once you fully comprehend with whom you are working, you can best structure solutions for their highly individualized needs. All of your library initiatives will be best received if they are presented as solutions to your users' problems.

2.) Learn to use your tools. Push word processing and spreadsheet tools beyond their basic usage, so that you can make strong arguments with your written and electronic documents. Take advantage of built-in graphics generators, such as Excel's ability to create bar graphs and pie charts from your data. Modify defaults to meet your needs so that you can be most efficient and can communicate most clearly. If you do not know how to use those tools, learn—either with a book, in a class, or from your peers.

3.) Remain aware of vendors, vendor mergers, new tools, and retiring old tools. Resource costs will inevitably rise, but you can consistently place your firm in its best position if you are aware of alternatives. Know which products you have already purchased, and review your licenses to determine if you are allowed access to print reinforcements, daily updates, distribution tools, etc. Be aware of competitors to your current vendors, and do not be afraid to consider switching products if there is a real and substantial cost advantage.

4.) Recognize training opportunities wherever they arise, creating new ones where possible. The days of sponsoring a lunch and seeing two dozen eager attentive faces sitting around the table are mostly gone. Take every chance you can to educate users; for example, stop by their offices to drop off print materials. Offer to show them how to find electronic resources, traveling to their offices so that they can use their own computers and customize their own desktops. Recognize that some users will learn best if they have print supplementation of your instructions; others will need to operate the mouse and work through the research on their own. Always explain how you are doing what you do, even if someone is just looking over your shoulder as you pull an "easy" document.

Law schools have never emphasized legal research; instead, they focus on learning problem-solving strategies, supported by the specific facts of individual cases. As formal curricula become more and more specialized, there is less and less time for students to learn the basics of legal research. Even schools that boast strong research classes tend to offer those to first-year students, newly minted law school students who do not have a frame of reference for most questions they learn to answer. Anticipate that first-year associates must be taught how to research from the ground up, throwing out their general inclination to believe that all information is available for free through Google. Build on those junior associates' familiarity and comfort with online searching to teach them specific information gathering strategies.

5.) Use the language of business, applying it to your firm's financial goals. Do not be afraid of business management concepts such as "best practices" or accounting terms such as "departmental income statements." Create strategic plans and annual reports, showing how your library contributes to the underlying mission of your law firm. Modify your materials as new business concepts become popular, adapting to current "buzzwords" to reflect your engagement with your firm's long-term business health.

Benchmarking Procedures

Managers need to evaluate consistently whether their actions are successful. Success can be measured in many different ways, but it must be measured and reported on, so that the library is consistently viewed as an entity that can set and meet goals, furthering the mission of the law firm.

Specifics will vary from goal to goal, but the principle remains the same. Managers should define the goal and then develop concrete benchmarks. They should measure their progress against those benchmarks on a regular, pre-determined basis.

For example, a firm might want to maximize its users' efficiency at conducting searches on Westlaw. The library manager should define "maximum efficiency," determining specific measurements that are meaningful to the firm, including reduced number of searches, limitation of searches to the most specific database available, reduced cost of searches run, etc. The manager should structure a program to achieve those goals, determining how to train users, relying on in-library resources, other in-firm resources, vendors' representatives, and other means. After a set time interval, the library should assess users' behavior, analyzing users' search patterns to determine whether the initial goals have been met. If the goals have not yet been achieved, then alternative training should be developed.

Whenever possible, measure your results in dollars. For example, if you engage in a project to cancel twenty print titles from your collection, update management on your success by translating those cancellations into concrete dollars and cents. Firm management will almost certainly not care that you have returned ten volumes; they will take notice, though, that you have saved $500, in keeping with best practices, as incorporated into your strategic plan.

All too often, firms develop grand plans, but do not define success or measure themselves against that success. When a library achieves success it should advertise that achievement, reporting to firm management and users, and leveraging one successful campaign to launch the next.

Meeting Challenges

While virtually every area of law presents its unique challenges to library management, the greatest challenges are presented by practice groups that are very small or rather tangential to a law firm's main business. If a firm has a handful of primary practice groups, it can develop a depth of resources in those areas; some redundancy is rewarded as practitioners explore novel issues of law. The cost per practitioner remains relatively low.

If, however, a library is required to support ten individuals, each of whom has a separate practice area, the relative cost of that support rises. Specialized treatises are required for each area of law. While "umbrella" resources, such as Westlaw or LexisNexis, defray some of that cost, users inevitably require some specialized materials—materials that are costly to acquire, time consuming to master, and expensive to maintain. Nevertheless, library managers must strive to meet the diverse needs of their growing, specializing attorneys, paralegals, and staff.

Helpful Associations or Entities

Traditionally, law firm librarians joined the American Association of Law Libraries and/or its local chapters, such as the Law Librarians Society of DC. However, now that law firm librarians are increasingly facing a business environment that is more akin to that which exists in corporations, many librarians are finding support in the Special Libraries Association, including its local chapters, divisions, and caucuses.

These associations continue to remain important, both for their in-person meetings (annual meetings as well as local ones) and for their listservs. Contemporary networking is largely electronic, and the traditional associations allow cost-effective ways to accomplish working with our peers.

Other entities are emerging as valuable tools for librarians. The International Legal Technology Association, long considered a bastion of information for high-tech information "IT" types, offers listservs rich in technical information for librarians, including forums dedicated to knowledge management, maximizing computer applications such as Word and Excel and other "techie" matters. While it is sometimes necessary to remind more tech-minded peers of the importance of libraries, the exchange of information through these traditionally high-tech forums is invaluable.

Adapting to a Changing Role

The most important advice that I could give to a law firm librarian who is trying to adapt to his or her changing role is to keep in mind that change is constant. The specific points raised in this article today will likely be moot in five years. Specific resources come and go, individual attorneys arrive and depart, and entire law firms merge and splinter off.

Strategies survive, however. Critical examination of problems works, no matter what specific challenges are presented. Structured solutions, including measurable benchmarks, apply no matter what specific issue triggers the crafting of the solution.

Librarians should take care not to over-invest in any given solution. Vendors can be purchased; business partners can be knocked out of business overnight. By staying flexible, remaining involved in a community of librarians, and constantly assessing and reassessing users' needs, library managers will guarantee themselves a place at the law firm management table for decades to come.

Mindy Maddrey was an intellectual property litigator at a major Washington law firm for seven years, before she decided to become a law librarian. After earning her Masters in Science in information science at Catholic University during a hectic two-semester span, Ms. Maddrey returned to the firm where she had practiced, managing their reference services for seven years. She has been a library director for four years, most recently at Sonnenschein Nath & Rosenthal LLP. When she is not busy managing her active and diverse staff, Ms. Maddrey writes novels under her maiden name, Mindy Klasky.

Dedication: *She dedicates this article to her first library boss and ongoing library mentor, Robert Dickey of Arent Fox.*

Providing Value in the Legal Industry Today

Anne Stemlar
Director of Research and Library Services
Goodwin Procter LLP

Introduction

Research and law librarians have always played a key role in law firms and in the legal industry more generally. The legal profession is an "information rich" industry where quality research is necessary to solve complex legal problems. Law librarians are equipped with a broad knowledge of legal and business information resources, and are experts in research strategies; therefore, they can quickly navigate the complex web of legal information available, including constitutions, regulations, statutes, and case law. They are also able to direct users to quality and cost-effective research solutions. Law librarians have always done more than just organize books on the shelf—they know what is inside the books, and they know when and where that information will be relevant.

The role of law librarianship has gone through a sea change in recent times due to the rapid rise and availability of information resources online, the appearance of Web 2.0 technologies, and the increasingly competitive nature of the law firm industry.

The New Availability of Information

Increased availability of information on the Internet has revolutionized the way attorneys find and use information. Most attorneys are comfortable using the Internet and online research services. Many attorneys, though, have not necessarily become better consumers when it comes to choosing the "best" information resources. The law librarian's role as cost-efficient researcher and facilitator of research has grown to fill this gap between available information and the necessary abilities to sort through it. Today's law librarians are required to possess a deeper knowledge of research services than in times past; they must now be familiar with both print and electronic resources, and must have keen research skills in order to balance the abundance of information, and to choose the best source for the research project.

Many law firm librarians are finding their services need to expand beyond the traditional library setting. Law librarians are leaders or active participants in law firm knowledge management initiatives, conflicts and records management, marketing and competitive intelligence departments, intranet design and development, and are called in to contribute in firm-management projects including employee engagement and employee professional development and training. Law library administrators must manage the resources of their department, but also are expected to contribute and act as problem solvers and business leaders within the larger law firm.

Web 2.0 & New Technology

Due to the glut of information exchanged via e-mail alone, there is a greater demand to introduce technologies that help manage the problem of information overload. Information overload is a significant nuisance to law firms because it creates inefficiencies, and therefore causes the organization to be less productive.

RSS feeds and readers that help organize news, systems that manage electronic newsletters, and password management systems that are being introduced on the desktop are examples of technology solutions that help solve the problem of information overload.

Web 2.0 technologies, such as wikis and blogs, are also becoming popular as tools to exchange information and to collaborate on projects. RSS feeds and readers can be used in conjunction with wiki's and blogs. If a wiki, blog, or internal Web page has RSS functionality, firm members can instantly be notified when changes have been made to the content and no longer have to go back to a source time and time again scanning for new information. This saves firm members time, therefore increasing efficiency and productivity.

Password management systems can also help increase efficiency by organizing passwords for online services and databases such as Westlaw and Lexis. Some attorneys may have ten or more passwords to various research services; passwords are often lost or forgotten and this creates problems if a researcher needs immediate access to a service. We have tackled the problem in several ways. First, we have developed an internal password database using SQL. Our SQL password database provides librarians with an easy-to-use platform where they can quickly identify passwords assigned to an individual member of the firm. The internal database also provides detailed licensing information about the firm's electronic subscriptions whereby a librarian can quickly determine how a product is licensed and who may access the service. Second, we are in the process of implementing software that permits users to log in to a research platform using *one* password; the software will recognize the user and authenticate their log-in credentials for *all* of the research services that they can access. One log-in instead of ten log-ins! Both approaches are examples of how technology can solve simple yet complex problems.

Keeping Pace with the Law Firm Industry

Globalization of the legal industry, consolidation of law firms, and law firm mergers are also major factors that are shaping the way law firm libraries are providing service. A law firm library must be prepared to provide service to members of the firm who are not located at the same physical location, or who may even be working in a different time zone. Staffing the reference desk at all hours, troubleshooting technology problems from a distance, managing staff remotely and licensing electronic subscriptions for multiple offices in several countries are just a few of the issues that globalization is creating.

A major question associated with law firm globalization is the issue of whether to centralize or decentralize various services provided by the library. For example, does the firm staff a librarian in the Hong Kong office or are members of the Hong Kong office supported by library staff physically located in Boston? If reference services are handled only via e-mail, does the quality of research improve or does quality suffer because there is no personal interaction between librarian and researcher? There are no easy answers to these questions and generally, those in smaller offices learn to use e-mail, online research services, electronic databases, and internal databases of work product to complete most of their research. The decision of "when" to add a new staff member in a remote office can be aided by keeping detailed statistics of research requests. Research statistics can track the office location of the requestor, the time of the request, and the substantive nature of the question. A careful analysis of statistical trends can help pinpoint heavy users of library services and help identify where additional resources are needed.

The Response to New Technologies

I believe the response to new technologies has been mixed within the law librarianship community. While almost all law librarians are extremely comfortable with online research systems, many have not fully grasped the potential of incorporating new technologies when it comes to managing the delivery of information. A recent, informal survey conducted by the Association of Boston Law Librarians, found that only three of twenty-two responding law firm libraries are currently using a wiki. Furthermore, of the nineteen libraries that do not currently use a wiki, most "do not have plans to institute a wiki in the near future."[1] I feel that it is vital for law librarians to provide leadership when it comes to managing the firm's intranet, participating in knowledge management initiatives, incorporating Web 2.0 technologies into the law firm, and streamlining information delivery on the desktop. If librarians fail to step in and provide leadership in these areas, other departments within the institution will do so and this will eventually diminish the value of the library within the overall organization.

Legal Concerns in the Law Library

The two primary legal issues I deal with most frequently are copyright and licensing. Copyright compliance has always been important to law firms, but managing electronic copyright compliance is a complex issue. For example, law firm internal intranets are ripe for copyright violations since they are platforms where members of the firm are encouraged to contribute information and to collaborate on projects. As technology makes it easier for firm members to collaborate, it also becomes easier for members of the firm to unknowingly post and make available information that is covered by copyright or not properly licensed for distribution.

A law librarian's job is to make the institution aware of copyright issues as it relates to print and electronic information, to be a leader when it comes to creating and enforcing internal copyright policies and compliance guidelines, to educate individual members of the law firm about copyright,

---

[1] Carolyn Trask, "Wiki: A Knowledge-Sharing Tool Worth Embracing?" *ABLL Advocate*, Volume 31, Issue 2, Nov.-Dec. 2007, at 9, 11.

and to create an internal environment where copyright laws are enforced without inefficiency.

Proper licensing of electronic resources is an important component of this. Law librarians need to negotiate effective, multi-office license agreements for electronic subscriptions while balancing costs of these services. It is also vital that law librarians explain the scope of each license to users of electronic products and to be clear on what the current license allows and prohibits.

Law firms are very budget conscious, therefore it is necessary to systematically review all licenses to be sure the institution is paying for what it is using and to cancel services that are no longer relevant.

A particular troubling new trend is for vendors to license research products or subscriptions only at the "enterprise level." This creates a situation in which large law firms are paying more for a product than small law firms, simply because they have more attorneys, even in the case where large law firms do not use the product more than their smaller competitors. The challenge is to negotiate with vendors in order to get the best price or to creatively leverage several products to come up with a comprehensive research solution.

Providing Excellent Service

Attorneys value high-quality, cost-effective research solutions, especially when the solution is delivered in a short amount of time. Attorneys also value exceptional customer service.

A major role of the law library director is that of the full-time marketer. The most important message for this person to get across to the attorneys is that the librarians at the firm will add value to a research project as well as save them time and reduce their clients' research costs.

I have a detailed marketing plan that I developed with a member of my firm's marketing department. We sat down and discussed the goals of the library, reviewed my long- and short-term strategic plan, and brainstormed on how best to deliver my message and accomplish the department's goals.

My marketing approach has been very focused. As I am also new to my law firm, I felt members of the firm needed to better understand that the firm's librarians do more than just "find" items that they had already identified through their own research. My marketing efforts have been focused on changing this perception by promoting the firm's librarians as "partners in research," as "problem solvers" rather than just "finders" of previously identified information.

We incorporate our problem solving approach to research into all of the classes, presentations, and communications that are sent out of the library. This idea also aligns nicely with our firm's values of "client service" and collaboration. It is very important that the goals and strategy of a law firm library mirror those of the institution. It is becoming more common for law firm libraries to have strategic plans—it is not as common for law firm libraries to have strategic marketing plans. I think both types of plans are vital to ensuring the long-term survival of librarians in law firms.

Communication

The most difficult message to convey to attorneys is that a "free" resource is not always the "best" resource to be used in solving a research problem. Cost of research has always been a concern at law firms, and the Internet has certainly revolutionized how we find some types of information. For example, government reports, court dockets, and legislative information can easily be found on the Internet—this has saved us time, and has helped to control research costs. However, the legal research questions attorneys deal with are complex—if our clients' questions were not complex, they would not require our services.

Therefore, law librarians need to constantly stress that "quality" information is required when conducting research, because the conclusions based on that research will be used to advise clients, and our clients will use that advice to make business decisions. Sometimes "quality" information comes at a cost—but "quality" information is absolutely essential because our research needs to be 100 percent accurate.

This concept is often more difficult for our younger attorneys to accept. They are more comfortable with online resources and using the Internet, but they are also generally less equipped to evaluate the quality of an information source. To combat that, we focus our initial training courses on changing their mindset from relying on the Internet to relying on premium information that the firm provides to them, and stress that the firm librarian will help them develop the best research strategy to solve their research problem. Research training classes are developed around a specific research question where attorneys are asked to solve the problem by using the Internet, a treatise, an online service or a database of internal work product. By comparing all of these sources side by side, young attorneys can see that a strategic approach of relying on quality internal resources delivers a more focused, cost-effective, final result than if they had wasted time surfing the Web.

Developing easy to use and focused intranet research pages also helps with promoting and reinforcing this concept. Our research pages are created for each legal practice area and highlight premium research sources. We train attorneys to use internal research pages before jumping onto the Internet. Our task-based research "quick tools" section helps attorneys easily complete repetitive research tasks such as finding a case decision or finding a definition, or patent. Our premium news, treatise, and database sections link to only those sources that are relevant to the legal practice area and we purposely exclude services that are not used frequently. This is very different from Web design of ten years ago, where research pages linked to everything and the kitchen sink—this perpetuated information overload. Simple, focused intranet research pages that anticipate the research needs of a legal practice area are better since the firm librarians filter the information and design research pages that present "quality" over quantity.

The Value of the Law Library

I think the biggest challenge facing law firm librarians today has to do with providing value to the institution as a whole. The Internet has changed the way people find information, and now everyone who uses the Internet thinks they are conducting "research." In actuality, research is not surfing the Web and finding quick answers. Research, especially in the legal profession, requires an understanding of the complex web of legal information as well as knowledge as to how laws and legal concepts intersect.

PROVIDING VALUE IN THE LEGAL INDUSTRY TODAY

In very cost-conscious law firms, the continued expense of a library collection and library staff might be questioned if decision makers do not understand how law firm librarians contribute in providing quality information retrieval and consumption. Therefore, it is vital that law firm librarians distinguish themselves as "the best" resource in the firm when it comes to solving research problems; they must be regarded as problem solvers and time savers.

The best way for a law librarian to raise the bar and add value is to develop their skills when it comes to using the "reference interview." In library school, we are taught that researchers enter a library with a preconceived idea of what sources they need to solve their research problem. We are also taught that our reference interview questions shouldn't be intrusive to the researcher. In some libraries, this creates a barrier to solving the research problem. However, the reference interview is very powerful in a private library where all questions are fair game and where there is little concern for the privacy of the researcher. As colleagues of the attorney, we are all held to the same level of confidentiality, and have the same goal of solving a research problem for our client. Attorneys are sometimes challenging to work with, but law librarians need to be comfortable asking detailed questions about the research problem, and must be prepared to suggest alternatives to the attorney's suggested approach. One way to develop the skills of the reference interview is to get in the habit of asking at least one question every time you have a research request. One question will quickly lead to two questions and eventually a detailed conversation about the problem the attorney is trying to solve will develop. If you have more details about the research problem, you will be better equipped to find a cost-effective and quality solution.

Tracking Value in the Library

It is difficult to measure empirically the success of a law library within its firm; kudos and praise are appreciated, but they are difficult to quantify. One way to monitor success is by keeping detailed research statistics. Research statistics track how many research requests are handled by a law library, and for a large law firm they can show which offices and which practice areas are using your services the most. If you are being successful, your statistics should be going up. Success is also demonstrated in return customers. Do attorneys come back as repeat customers?

You also know you are on the right track when the library receives invitations to present programs for a department, instead of the library requesting an audience at a department meeting.

The Jurisdiction of the Library

In many law firms, the jurisdiction of the law librarian has notably expanded in recent years. Every institution is different, however, when it comes to defining what this role is, and how far it goes. The determination of these boundaries has much to do with the organizational structure of the firm, and of course the position of the head librarian at the institution. For example, at my last law firm the law library director was in charge of the firm's intranet, extranets, firm knowledge management, research, and library services. At my current law firm, I have jurisdiction over research and library services, and I have the responsibility of working with the firm's knowledge management initiative, bringing a library science discipline to the team. My firm's intranet is officially under the IT department.

Many law libraries have jurisdiction over competitive intelligence research, while in some law firms this function is firmly located in the marketing department. I also participate in redesigning the firm's intranet, and contribute to HR initiatives that relate to on-boarding new employees, engaging current employees, and training and professional development of administrative employees. As a law firm administrator, I am required to contribute in more than just my main discipline of research and library services, and am expected to collaborate and contribute as a business leader in the law firm.

I think this is becoming a more common approach in law firms as they continue to grow and cross-disciplinary approaches to problem solving are adapted. Again, every institution is different, and in many institutions, librarians do not want to step out of the "traditional" role of the librarian and participate in other areas of the law firm. In my opinion, law librarians should grasp these new opportunities; when a law librarian leader is involved in any areas outside of the traditional library, this elevates and strengthens the library's position within the institution.

Adding Value through Collaboration

Law libraries in law firms will only continue to be successful if they build strong strategic relationships with other administrative departments within their organizations. Law libraries must develop particularly strong relationships with their IT departments in order to get necessary technical support in developing and maintaining new technologies. IT professionals can provide information on the organization's network capabilities and advice on necessary technical requirements when the library is purchasing new software. IT also provides the necessary technical support for the library's online catalog and is the source for keeping the library updated on changes to the firm's IP addresses and firewall. A good relationship between the two groups can keep library systems working smoothly.

Law librarians also need to take the lead in competitive intelligence and business development research for marketing departments. If they fail to take on this role, this type of research will be completed by the marketing department—or in some cases will be outsourced altogether.

The law library training curriculum should also incorporate knowledge management concepts. In order to develop strategic relationships with other departments, it is necessary to understand the roles of the other administrative departments within the law firm, and to understand their challenges. Once you understand the roles and the challenges faced by other administrative departments, you will find opportunities to promote your department while improving the service that the other departments offer.

Long-standing conflicts like billable hours and non-billable research costs need to be accepted as part of doing business for the firm—client development and competitive research is as vital to the firm as client work when it comes to the long-term viability of the institution and even more important in our highly competitive legal markets. A "one-firm" collaborative approach among administrative departments is necessary to compete in the current legal market. I believe it is within the scope of the law librarian's duty to assist and even lead in bringing together such a collaboratively successful environment.

Anne Stemlar joined Goodwin Procter in 2006 as the firm's director of research and library services. Prior to joining Goodwin Procter, Ms. Stemlar spent ten years with WilmerHale (formerly Hale and Dorr LLP). Starting as a reference librarian in 1996, she eventually became that firm's manager of research services, responsible for coordinating research training and research services across the firm's offices. Ms. Stemlar also held reference librarian positions at Peabody & Brown (now Nixon Peabody LLP) and Kasdorf, Lewis & Swietlik, SC. Ms. Stemlar is a frequent lecturer on legal research techniques and legal research training in law firms. She is a member of the State Bar of Wisconsin, American Association of Law Libraries, Law Librarians of New England, and the Association of Boston Law Librarians. Ms. Stemlar graduated from the University of Iowa with degrees in history and psychology, earned her J.D. from Marquette University Law School and earned an M.L.I.S. from the University of Wisconsin-Milwaukee.

The Proactive Law Librarian

Monice M. Kaczorowski
Director of Library Services
Neal, Gerber & Eisenberg LLP

Introduction

In order to thrive in the world of the modern law firm, librarians need to be proactive rather than reactive. They no longer have the luxury of waiting in the library for attorneys to seek out their services.

Proactive librarians publish monthly newsletters and place announcements on the library portal or Web page touting library services, attend attorney practice group meetings, and often partner with their firm's marketing department to assist in preparation of RFP and business development initiatives. These librarians make sure to be included in the orientation process for staff joining the firm, in order to advertise the library's services to all attorneys, and to reiterate the essential role of the law firm library. In the same vein, they seek out creative marketing opportunities for showcasing their library initiatives via media events as speakers and writers in their professional organizations and publications. Library directors who work closely with other departments, such as marketing, recruiting, and information services, need to seize opportunities presented to co-author articles or serve as co-panelists. These are excellent venues to showcase library initiatives to professional groups that may not realize the value of libraries in their own organizations.

National Library Week, which is an annual American Library Association sponsored event each April, is one chance to market your library's abilities to the people in your firm. You can use this time proactively to educate them on the power of the library, to showcase vendor and library services, or to host an event thanking the firm for helping the library help their attorneys. Use the event to leverage the most attractive aspects of your library.

Marketing to populations outside of your firm is also beneficial. One way to go about this is to sponsor a local organization with a "read event," either by donating money or books that are pertinent to the group, and to make sure everyone knows it was made possible by the library of your organization. This is a particularly great way to market the firm and the firm's library if a client is on the board of that organization.

The Evolving Law Library

Attorneys have traditionally relied on the library for general legal research, but that relationship has recently changed in several fundamental ways. Along with legal research, the library is now called upon to perform hot topic research for attorney blogs, due diligence on the creditworthiness of potential clients and outside vendors, assistance with article and speech preparation for media opportunities, and to produce competitive intelligence reports for the firm's business development initiatives. Many law firm libraries also provide their attorneys with media watch services on their clients and competitors, newly filed litigation (docket watches), and pending legislation effecting their area of practice.

The popularity of watch services has grown and as a result, vendors such as Lexis are offering specialized technology to streamline the watch process. New applications such as Lexis Publisher and Ozmosys allow a library to run an unlimited number of watches utilizing a library's subscription services to BNA, Westlaw, and Lexis. The watches can be set to run once a day, continually, or somewhere in between. The search results are then pushed to attorney e-mail, the web portal, or an RSS feed, as designated when the search is set up. These watches can be branded with the organization's logo and customized for client alerts. The library provides the current awareness service utilizing minimal amounts of staff time. Once the alerts are set up and tested, they virtually run on their own.

The law firm library today actively supports these objectives:

1. Facilitating legal research
2. Producing quality business intelligence
3. Promoting awareness of current events
4. Supporting media opportunities
5. Bolstering the firm's bottom line by supporting business development

Central to the objectives of the proactive librarian is the task of getting attorneys to think of the library as their "go-to" place for a variety of information. Librarians are highly educated professionals with subject expertise and excellent research skills; they are hired to support the practice of the attorney, and to improve the bottom line of the firm. The library, therefore, should not be an afterthought when it comes to any variety of informational requests, rather as an extremely useful resource, and librarians as experts in manipulating it to its best end.

As professionals, we contribute to the attorney work product with information that would be difficult for the attorney to glean on his or her own. The library's role in the firm is complementary, but absolutely essential, and the attorneys need to be reminded of this.

The law librarian facilitates cost-effective, client-related legal research. Legal materials, and the sources used to access them, are in a constant state of flux. Online services change incessantly, but the librarian is in place to keep pace with this change. Librarians have to remain steadfast in order to get that message across. This implies retraining attorneys who—always driven by the billable hour—feel they learned everything about online searching in law school, and that they are smart enough to grasp things intuitively by simply signing on to the service.

1. Value of library service
2. Knowledge and expertise of librarians valuable enough to charge clients
3. Cost-effective legal research for attorneys

Attorneys are driven by the billable hour, and their time is extremely valuable. To persuade them to use more reliable and effective methods for gathering information requires making sure that messages from the library are brief, to the point, and not perceived as a waste of time. On the other hand, you have to stay on the attorney's radar screen, which means regular communication. To strike a balance, the librarian needs to always strive to establish a peer-to-peer relationship. At times, this can be difficult when dealing with a strong personality and billable hour demands, but it can and must be done. With a peer-to-peer relationship, attorneys get the best information, and the library maintains its deserved relevance in the firm.

Challenges Librarians Face

There are three primary challenges the law librarian must inevitably face, which are:

--Change management: This means being creative in adjusting library services as the needs of your organization change, as opposed to digging in your heels and continuing library services as they have always been.
--Staying on top of business concerns: Being fiscally responsible and possessing the business skills and sense to do so.
--Service implementation: Making choices that have a positive affect on the firm, and being willing to see processes through when you are challenged.

Change Management

Change management means surveying attorneys and staff on their perception of library service. In order to be as effective as possible, librarians need to find out what does and does not work. Draw up a survey. On this survey, it is helpful to provide a suggestion area for changes attorney and staff would like to see; once you know what these are, you should implement those changes and advertise and give credit to people responsible for the suggestions. Publish the results of the survey so that people who took the time to answer realize their opinions count. People are much more likely to respond a second time if they see that you have acknowledged their contribution the first time.

Also, find alternative ways to understand the firm's needs and demands. Spend time knocking on doors or using elevator encounters to find out what is going on with the practice groups and C-level people in your organization. Process this information into effective complimentary roles for the library. Make sure you know what your organization's business plan is for the next three to five years so that you can align your library business plan to reflect and actualize those goals.

Running Your Library like a Business

Nobody in your organization will fault you for being fiscally responsible when it comes to the library's budget. Do not shy away when you are asked to prepare a budget. Do not prepare it in a void, either. Make sure you talk to the CFO or comptroller and find out what months are cash rich for your organization so that your major invoices come due in those months. Look into special billing plans offered by vendors to streamline the invoice process. If you are able to stem the flurry of invoices and have your accounting department cut one check a month instead of forty for a single vendor, you have saved hours of staff time, which translates into dollars. If you do not have a clear understanding of accounting, then check out local classes held at a community college that will give you an overview of accounting and business practices, or look for a mentor in the accounting department at your firm. Talk to the head of your recruiting department to make sure you know what the firm is intending in terms of adding practice groups and personnel and what the impact will be on your budget.

Librarians have to negotiate major vendor contracts for very expensive online services and electronic library subscriptions. Make sure that your contracts for online services reflect the needs of your firm. If your needs change, do not live with an inadequate contract: renegotiate it so that it works for your firm. Once these contracts are in place, implement client matter validation products to capture research costs for client-related research.

Also implied in running your library like a business is tracking return on investment (ROI). Make sure that your accounting department provides you with monthly reports that enable you to track your costs against budget. These reports should give you the information needed to adjust your budget if errors occur. In regards to online usage, the accounting department should supply cost recovery and write up/down reports so that you can track recovery and contact attorneys that are writing off charges to educate them on the value of online services and billing for librarian time.

Implementing Services, Facing Challenges

Librarians are called upon to do what they feel is best for their organization, but they are also held responsible for the changes implemented. As librarians, we are in the best place to look at how our libraries fit into the big picture of our organization. The attorneys approving those changes often are senior management or executive committee level who typically are not heavy library users, including online services. More often than not, they are at a stage in their career where they delegate to others who use the library services. It is a good idea to keep all of this in mind.

Make sure your plans are carefully reasoned. If you want to make a major change, put it in the form of a business plan. What are the stages and what will the end result look like? How will the change add value to the organization? Being able to take responsibility if the plan fails, and being able to work on the project until you have achieved the desire result is all part of running your library like a business.

Benchmarking the Library's Success

You and your library are excelling in the law firm if:

1. You are perceived as the person who knows what is best for the library.
2. You are in your organization's "inner circle" and are routinely kept informed about changes affecting the firm so that you can be prepared to have the library support these changes.
3. You are viewed as fiscally responsible and the library budget is viewed as sound; therefore you are allowed to spend it as you see fit once approved for the year.
4. Attorneys listen to you when you explain why online charges should be passed on to the client, and why it is a sound business practice to do so (i.e., you are not giving the client a false sense of what it costs to represent them).
5. Your library is efficiently capturing client billables for attorney-related online services so that you can add additional online services to next year's budget.
6. Your librarian time is being billed and your staff is perceived as revenue generators; you are allowed to add staff as needed.

Training Issues

Along with general library training, librarians need to have a basic understanding of business, accounting, HR, communication skills, and IT knowledge. A well-managed law library represents a significant long-term investment within the law firm. You need an understanding of general business and accounting principles in order to communicate effectively with your accounting department. Rather than relying solely on HR—especially for firms doing business in multiple states and on an international level—

the librarian should have a basic understanding of workplace law and HR resources. As a librarian, you need to be able to get your message out and to communicate with your peers within the firm. Attorneys are schooled in negotiation and communication, and so should the librarian.

Because the library relies heavily on technology, forming a solid relationship with the information technology (IT) department is crucial. You should be able to communicate your technology needs to your IT department. Since many librarians report to IT directors, a basic knowledge of technology puts you in an advantageous peer-to-peer relationship. In order to help with this, librarians should seek out continuing education courses, association seminars, and memberships outside the field of librarianship to enhance their managerial skills.

Fifteen years ago, students were lucky if they were offered one very abstract course in administration in library school. Times have changed. Today librarians have to manage 24/7 virtual reference, negotiate million dollar site licenses for online services, and track cost recovery and return on investment. In the past, librarians were trained and were much more passive and reactive. Today, librarians must be proactive in order to be effective. Furthermore, they are expected to be experts in their field not only in terms of librarianship, but in some capacity also as a legal administrator, records manager, or conflicts manager.

In the past, having graduated from library school one chose to be in either reference or technical services. If you were a reference librarian, your career path was to head a department and eventually run a library. Now reference librarians have more opportunities to expand into roles in competitive intelligence, knowledge management or hold titles like E-librarians or Internet services specialist.

Previously, someone interested in technical services was a cataloger or acquisitions librarian. They stayed in the backroom having very little interaction with the public. Today, technical services librarians are electronic services librarians, Web masters, and portal page designers. They meet with vendors, negotiate contracts, and train library patrons. They create and administer firm Web pages and portals and interact with patrons as they design and test the friendliness of these products. In some cases today, there are those library positions that encompass library and marketing functions, or the library and IT, which was unheard of fifteen years ago. Law librarians today manage multiple departments within the firm, such as record, conflicts, and docket, as well as the library.

Financial Considerations

Succeeding in the field of librarianship today calls upon one to be fiscally responsible.

Being fiscally responsible includes:

1. Budgeting
2. Cost recovery
3. Salary negotiating
4. Return on investment for library services
5. Print versus electronic

Librarians must know how to prepare meaningful budgets. The library budget of today is much more detailed, reflecting the expense of salaries, print products, outside service costs, electronic subscriptions, and online services. In order to make library expense more palatable to management, it often helps to include projected revenue recovery for online services and library billables for that same fiscal year. By doing so, one presents the library budget in more realistic terms to management. It is prudent to set levels of recovery as an item in the library goals section and outline what objectives must be met to achieve cost recovery. In doing so, it shows management that the library budget is a tool to be used twelve months of the year.

The librarian should work closely with the CFO and firm comptroller in overseeing the budget. Once the budget is approved by management, the librarian should request monthly reports from accounting to make sure line items are accurate and that other departments or attorneys have not charged items inappropriately. Accounting should supply the librarian with monthly general ledger reports for budget monitoring. Also, librarians should receive monthly online database recovery reports as well as write up/write down reports on client charges and library time.

Librarians need to be mindful of tracking cost recovery for online services, and to take the initiative to instruct attorneys that are not clear on how these costs translate into effective research for their clients. For librarians that bill, the rates should reflect the level of librarian expertise, and librarians should communicate the value of that research so that they do not become the victims of write-offs or write-downs. If clients have an issue with billing for librarian time, then meet with accounting and see if they are willing to change your title to senior information professional. Sometimes a simple change of title on a client's bill can make a difference in how your work is perceived. It is important to keep client engagement letters current and make sure they reflect the current discounts passed on to clients in terms of online contracts with Lexis and Westlaw or other major online vendors.

Non-billable time can be just as valuable to the firm as time billed to clients. Librarians who work with marketing to help prepare RFPs and support practice development initiatives are helping to bring in new clients and increase revenue, hence positively effecting the firm's bottom line. Rather than lump all non-billable research into one category, spend some time with your accounting department and create specific matter numbers that are reflective of the work being done. This billing detail will help one better analyze time in terms of how exactly library time is being spent.

Librarians also need to be good at negotiating salaries for their staff. Salaries ought to reflect market value for the services provided, and should not cave into minimal increases because of past payment precedents. Each librarian should set goals and objectives for themselves on an annual basis including billable hours. Breaking down billables per month makes them less daunting and more easily achievable. These goals should be reviewed quarterly to make sure staff is on track. At the end of the year, these goals and objectives hopefully have turned into accomplishments and will play a significant role in year-end reviews along with salary surveys from both local and national legal and librarian associations. Association memberships and opportunities for continuing education in the upcoming year should be considered when negotiating year-end increases for library staff.

When measuring return on investment for library services, these days law firms are looking beyond library billables and cost recovery for client-related research and on to the expense of maintaining print collections. The cost of print is two-fold—the price of the subscription and processing along with the cost of real estate for housing the collection. Librarians are being asked to take a hard look at what it costs to support a practice group in terms of materials in the collection and office copy expense. The need for reported information is becoming much more detailed. This information is time consuming to compile. One should not wait to be asked, but rather be proactive in working with technical services staff to put software systems in place to track this data so that reports can be generated.

If asked, librarians should be able to supply reports to management that reflect the cost of supporting any practice group in the firm. Providing this information will allow a practice group leader to make intelligent decisions on what materials are necessary to support the group practice. This is often the time the library is approached about canceling print material and moving to an electronic format, which isn't always a cheaper solution.

In terms of electronic subscriptions, one should consider both the cost and convenience for attorneys. This will be a major change in the way attorneys and staff access the library. For multi-generational patrons, the first electronic subscription can either make or break the perception of how the library delivers information. One needs to carefully weigh all the options and not just consider the cost of the product. An IP authenticated site license can be more expensive, but in the long run can prove more cost effective than multiple copies of a print source that are never on the shelf or lost in the routing process. Electronic subscriptions can be made available via the library Web page or portal and can be easily accessed by an attorney at their desk, at home or in court. With IP authentication, there are no additional passwords to remember and the access is seamless for every user regardless of location.

With new software available such as Onelog, a librarian can easily track the usage patterns of any online subscription and produce detailed reports to support either the continuation or cancellation of any electronic subscription. Unlike books that have a hit or miss tracking system through the circulation process, electronic subscriptions are easily tracked. They are perfect candidates for cancellations if little used and the proof is in the usage tracking so when an attorney complains that they use it everyday, you will have solid proof to support your collection development decisions. With the proper training aids in place for the switch in formats, electronic subscriptions might be a way to reconfigure collection space and turn shelving into revenue-generating cubicles for additional reference staff.

National surveys put the cost of libraries at generally 3 to 5 percent of overall law firm expense. Librarians need to be mindful of where they fit into the overall structure of the law firm and the role the library plays in law firm profitability. The librarian should always be prepared when asked to produce a report on cost recovery, library billables, or the cost of supporting practice groups in the firm. This is all part of being a fiscally responsible librarian.

Conclusion

It is critical for the modern librarian to take out time to learn the business of law, and to understand how your particular organization functions. You need to find your organization's three to five year business plan, understand where you fit within it, and what you can do to support the specified initiatives. Also, it is essential that the librarian gain top management support for the library, and work with their fellow departmental directors in supporting each other and your organization. Be on a first name basis with the executives in your firm, and strive for effective communication.

Information is power. When you have the ear of the executives in your organization, and you supply them with cutting-edge news and business intelligence, you are part of the team that helps run the firm. Instead of being in a support staff role, you have moved up to the C-suite and become a peer to those running the firm.

The library cannot exist in a vacuum. You may have the best intentions as a librarian, and an agenda that you feel is important, yet you may be in conflict as to where your organization is headed. As the resident information professional, you need to be proactive in providing your organization with the research and information necessary in furthering their goals. No one in your organization is better placed than the librarian as an information provider in assisting management, providing current awareness, and gathering business intelligence.

Librarians can no longer be passive. They have to be agents for change. They have to be on the front lines supporting and promoting their organization to colleagues and their clients.

Monice M. Kaczorowski has been director of library services for Neal, Gerber & Eisenberg LLP since June 2003. Prior to joining the firm, she was director of libraries for Ross & Hardies for fourteen years. She works closely with the marketing department and attends monthly practice group meetings to develop needs assessments and to promote business development within the firm. Ms. Kaczorowski has created a Competitive Intelligence Unit within the library that supports the firm's practice development efforts and RFP process. Ms. Kaczorowski continues to work with the firm's legal education committee and has developed a new associate legal research training program.

Ms. Kaczorowski's professional affiliations include memberships in the Special Libraries Association (SLA), Chicago Association of Law Libraries (CALL) and American Association of Law Libraries (AALL). She is a past member of the WEST Advisory 2002-2004.

Ms. Kaczorowski is the author of numerous articles and has spoken frequently on the topic of law firm library management. She earned her B.A. from St. Mary's College, Notre Dame, Indiana, and her M.L.S. from Dominican University.

Acknowledgements: *I would like to thank Joseph M. Milligan, director of client services and marketing, Neal, Gerber & Eisenberg LLP for his editorial assistance and Tracey E. Smith for her discerning eye on librarianship.*

Key Elements in the Law Firm Librarian's Changing Role

Mary Kay Jung
Director of Library Services
Thompson Coburn LLP

The Changing Role of Law Firm Librarianship

As few as twenty years ago the law firm library was the firm's showcase—a physically impressive wood and leather decorated room with large collections of books that supported the practices of the firm (and looked good on the shelves). Our firm, for example, had four sets of the Missouri, Illinois, and U.S. codes, the full National Reporter set, duplicate copies of the Missouri, Illinois, and federal cases and innumerable multi-volume loose-leafs and treatises, all of which were kept up to date with frequent filings, supplements, or pocket-parts. Attorneys worked at one of fourteen tables in the library where several books could be spread out and where the librarian was available to assist in using the materials or to direct the user to the best resource. Lexis and Westlaw were accessed through dedicated terminals and used infrequently because of the perception of their high cost to a client. Due to the sheer number of physical volumes, much of the library staff's time was spent on collection maintenance: material check-in, cataloging, processing, and shelving of the books. Library staff also pulled, copied, and Shepardized cases, compiled legislative histories, and instructed the newer attorneys on the use of the paper collection.

Since then, with the availability of the personal computer, wide area networks, and a reliable Internet connection, nearly all current legal materials have become available electronically. More cases, statutes, and digests than any physical library could hold are available on the attorney's desktop. Services formerly used in loose-leaf or treatise format are now online with updates available immediately. Newsletters are delivered by e-mail and include links to the full-text of related materials. Attorneys conduct most of their legal research in their offices. Lexis and Westlaw contracts are negotiated to fixed costs and the online services are often the starting point of research.

These changes in the library have changed the role of law librarians. Less time is spent on processing and shelving materials. Pulling and Shepardizing cases can be done with a few keystrokes. Library patrons who need help may well be in another time zone as they contact the library staff by e-mail or phone call. While attorneys still do their own legal research, they rely on the librarian for answers to complex questions and for non-legal research. Librarians provide medical, scientific, and business research. They may conduct business intelligence on clients or competitors. They are responsible for organizing the numerous electronic resources so attorneys can find the best product when they need it and make sure the log-on credentials associated with each resource are available 24/7. Librarians manage their firm's knowledge management initiatives, deliver current awareness on clients and industries, and collaborate with other administrative departments on tools for business development and internal communication.

Changing Procedures

To provide these new services, librarians have had to employ the available technology to streamline paper-based procedures and to enable access to the electronic materials. Catalogs are now electronic, probably Web-based, and encompass the online collection as well as the paper. The new library catalog doesn't merely mimic the old card catalog, but also provides new access points not available in the paper card catalog such as links to tables of contents, indices, author biographies, and chapter summaries. Current awareness services extend beyond newsletter routing and include compiling value-added lists of articles relevant to an industry, a practice area or client. Verifying and re-evaluating Internet links in alphabetical and topical lists is done in concert with shelf reading to ensure users can find what they need, no matter its format. Having come to terms with the fact that the younger attorneys do not use the paper collection as extensively as their predecessors did, librarians now find other ways to supply the peripheral information reading the books or browsing the shelves used to provide. This includes organizing the electronic resources topically, using the firm's intranet to group related materials, and providing access to firm-wide work product in an easily accessible collection.

Identifying and Developing New Procedures and Practices for Librarianship

Improving procedures and adding services is a constant in library services and inspiration for a new procedure comes about in a variety of ways. Sometimes a new technology is the trigger. When desktop scanning became available, the technical services staff quickly seized on the idea of scanning and e-mailing journal tables of contents (TOCs) to replace the existing photocopy and manual delivery of the TOCs. Sometimes a new procedure is needed to provide a service. As more and more research products required unique user IDs and passwords, we found we were answering an exponential number of calls for users' log-on information. We created a database of the resource links to which we now associate each user's log-on credentials as they are received. When the user hovers over the link, his log-on information is revealed (without a call to the library). This same database is used to populate the alphabetical and topical Internet indices, enabling entering or editing the link a single time no matter the number of pages on which it will appear. Still other times, demands for a new library service will suggest a new process as with the creation of our electronic clipping service tool, the Headlines Publisher. Its development was necessary in order to keep up with the increasing number of requests from attorneys for additional headlines to monitor clients and industries and the library's desire to provide the headlines in a consistent format. Our need to be certain we are providing the right resources required we find some process to check usage on our electronic titles in the same way our re-shelving statistics provided usage data on the books.

Marketing the Services of the Firm's Library

Providing new services can't be done in a vacuum and we rely on internal marketing to update attorneys on new library services. Our tactics involve using every resource at hand—a library template to create and generate our client and industry headlines that states on every page that this is "a service of the Thompson Coburn Library"; our intranet page to highlight library staff and services; and a weekly "Do You Know?" e-mail to introduce new or underutilized library resources. We hand deliver requested research and interlibrary loans to personalize the experience and, with the help of our media department, create American Library Association-like READ posters featuring pictures of firm attorneys and staff with their favorite books to celebrate National Library Week. When rolling out a major new product, we create entire campaigns that include thematic intranet banners, posters, and gifts delivered to the attorneys and staff.

Changes to Financial and Technological Elements of Librarianship

With new technology comes new challenges and one of the most taxing areas is cost. Managing the library budget was less complex when the collection was largely paper and the use of a database like Lexis or Westlaw could be charged back in full to the client. The cost of paper was fixed (who negotiated how much they would pay for the Standard Federal Tax Reporter?) and the only discounts offered were for multiple copies of the same title. When titles first became available in electronic format, common practice was to offer the title in paper or in electronic format, not in both. It was not unusual to pay for a new electronic title by canceling an equivalent cost in paper titles. Publishers quickly developed pricing structures that offered the electronic version at a discounted cost if the paper was also maintained. That effectively removed the incentive to cancel the paper, but offered no resolution to the problem of the increased costs of maintaining duplicate formats. Librarians struggle with balancing the collection between paper and electronic titles, especially in multi-office firms, where the cost for enterprise-wide licensing can be many times the cost of a paper subscription per office. In some circumstances, generational preferences for the paper or electronic version make it politically impossible to rely on a single format.

It is not only the online costs that are rising at a rate much higher than inflation. Monographs, journals, supplements, and loose-leaf titles in paper increased by as much as 10 percent in 2007. At least one enterprising publisher has begun offering a Library Maintenance Agreement (LMA), which will hold inflation closer to 5 percent, but only if the subscribing library agrees that it will not cancel more than 5 percent of its existing subscriptions. Entering into such an LMA will control paper costs but eliminates the incentive to cancel lesser used titles.

With increased costs limiting the number of new titles purchased, librarians are evaluating different technologies as vehicles to provide new services. The criteria used for new services include present or anticipated need, usability, universality, training requirement, and cost-benefit. Ultimately, if it does not make it easier, better or faster to do the job or to provide a new service, there is no reason to invest time or money in a new technology. Some products currently being considered for library applications are podcasting and blogging to update users on new resources or to replace the "Do You Know?" services; federated searching, Google toolbar, and tagging to improve or replace the library catalog; library-created RSS feeds for current awareness services; and wiki software for the reference database.

When developing new services, attention must be given to two particularly difficult legal issues related to information delivery—digital copyright and licensing of online resources. Librarians have always had a role in making sure the firms' copying fell under the fair use guidelines. When we were concerned only with copying paper, we would feel we were complying—at least with the spirit of the law—if we convinced our firms to get a license with the Copyright Clearance Center (CCC) which covered most of our titles. Reproduction of material delivered electronically is a new area that seems more complex, at least to this librarian. And while the CCC offers a digital license, it covers very few titles that we need. The scope of what we are allowed to reproduce is affected by the licensing of our electronic media. The challenges to librarians include understanding what we can legally send electronically to our attorneys and to our clients under our agreements, and educating the attorneys on what they can forward or post. We must also know *how* to license, whether by practice area, by location, or across the enterprise.

Overcoming the Challenges for Today's Law Firm Librarians

A fundamental challenge in today's law firm environment is to ensure others in our firm see us outside of the stereotypical librarian role and outside of the library. We need to make sure we are using our skills where they can have the greatest impact on the firm, whether it is directly with attorneys or with administrative departments such as business development, finance, human resources, or information technology. We need to be aggressive in keeping up with the changes in the legal industry and with the developments in technology so we can apply them to library services. We must be less traditional and more entrepreneurial in our thinking. Who better than the library director to explain to the relationship partner the value of business analysis of his top clients and their industries? Who better than the library to show the marketing department how we can push company news to the Client Relationship Manager (CRM)? Librarians can gather information for the executive director on potential merger targets, and for HR on lateral attorneys in practice areas where the firm is expanding. They can find the best CLE programs for professional development and teach the newest partners how to find business development opportunities. Once librarians understand how they can help, they have to go where the need is—practice area meetings, administrative departmental meetings, etc., and let the end user know how they can help.

Another challenge is resistance to change at all levels of the firm. Library staff members who are fearful they are not up to the technological challenge must be shown their traditional skills are still needed, just in a more automated setting. Senior partners refusing to accept the associates' online research as complete need to understand the depth of the research performed. Associates relying only on online tools must be shown what traditional research might uncover. The library director should position herself to provide guidance in any circumstance where her knowledge of information and research can alleviate concerns and educate the end user.

Training for the Next Generation of Law Firm Librarians

The next generation of law firm librarians will face many of the same challenges current librarians face: working with multi-generational staffs and patrons, balancing the collection between paper and electronic, handling contract negotiations, and employing evolving technology to deliver information better and more quickly. In addition, a significant number of these librarians will be working in global law firms, which will pose additional layers of complexity in working across international time zones and in offices where different languages are spoken.

Because information and information technology were being revolutionized while I've been in the field, I had the luxury of learning on the job. In 1989, even if law firm management had an inkling that the Internet existed, no one had any sense of the monumental changes it would be responsible for in delivering information. I was able to migrate from a two Lexis UBIQ library to a wide-area networked PC environment incrementally and over time, learning the nuances of contract negotiations and licensing gradually. The next generation of law firm librarians will be expected to know much more about technology, the impact of licensing decisions, and law firm financials upon getting that first job.

Skills Necessary at a Law Firm

Because libraries and library services will always be centered on information, the traditional librarianship skills of information organization, delivery, and research will always be a part of the job. But libraries are no longer independent, self-sufficient entities, and in order to function completely within the larger organization, knowledge of management practices, information technology, and information analysis are needed. Librarians must understand the mission and goals of their law firm and work as part of an administrative team to foster these missions and goals. Librarians most certainly have to shake the stereotype of the quiet, non-assertive book shuffler and become a force outside of the library walls who contributes to the bottom line and to the firm's culture.

Traditional library skills are learned in ALA-accredited library schools, but they must make certain that they keep up with the needs of special librarians. Choosing librarianship as a career means choosing a lifetime of continuing education. Excellent programs are offered at annual meetings of professional associations such as the American Library Association, Special Library Association, American Association of Law Libraries, and Society of Competitive Intelligence Professionals, as well as the state and regional chapters of these groups. Other organizations, such as Practising Law Institute, offer programs specific to law librarianship and at least two of the major providers of legal information, LexisNexis and Thomson West, offer innovative workshops for law librarians. In addition, the literature of the legal profession and the information industry should be considered required reading.

Conclusion

Law is a knowledge-based profession and, as such, will continue to rely on information. Librarians who promote the library as a series of information services and not a room full of books position themselves to be an integral part of the law firm for years to come.

Mary Kay Jung has been the director of library services at Thompson Coburn LLP since 1989. Prior to her work at the law firm, she was the deputy circuit librarian at the U.S. Court of Appeals for the Eighth Circuit. She has a B.A. from Benedictine College and an M.L.S. from Emporia State University.

Librarianship: A Profession in Transition

Linda Will
Director of Information Services
Dorsey & Whitney

Tradition Impacted by Technology and Global Competition

Traditionally, librarians have been the administrators of a law firm's scholarly resources, as well as the custodians of a firm's explicit external knowledge, meaning any resources that are purchased as opposed to the internal knowledge that comprises the work product a firm produces for its clients. Years ago, law firm librarians tended to stay hidden behind the ivy walls of their firm libraries, but in the last decade our role has altered in such a way that we are no longer ancillary; in fact, we are far more interactive with the other departments in our firms. This turnaround occurred because law firms have found that they can leverage their resources in a more fiscally responsible manner by using librarians in that way. Ultimately, every action in this economy is bottom line driven, so finances have been a strong catalyst for the transition of the traditional librarian role. The librarian's role has evolved from primarily managing external information to one that is increasingly involved with the firm's internal activities through interaction with other departments, such as marketing. For example, librarians often bring in the external information used by a marketing department's customer relationship management (CRM) programs. We are able to obtain the latest, most competitive intelligence; rather than simply data dumping, we are providing information that has been fully analyzed and can be used by the firm to make strategic decisions. Law firm librarians have embraced the new technologies and research tools that are now available to them, because they are increasingly viewed as a law firm's main conduit of information.

The most profound impact to the traditional role of librarianship has been caused by evolving technology. Technology touches everyone and has been the catalyst for global competition. From a research perspective, technology has been an equalizer, permitting masses of users access to the same sophisticated information. With the onset of the Information Revolution, hundreds of database and online resources sprung up. Consolidation in the industry, which both preceded and followed the technological revolution, brought challenges to purchasers of information services. However, we are now seeing a new trend emerge: the independents are breaking ties with aggregators and entering into law firm contracts on their own terms. This can present its own challenges as these entities are confident in the value of their information and therefore charge a premium for it.

Law firms spend a good deal of money on information services.; as such, this makes the administration of a firm's resources more of a challenge than ever. Technology never simply goes away; rather, it evolves. Now we have the Net generation of librarians who are not just controlling content but creating content. Many law librarians are in charge or part of the administrative team that oversees a firm's KM or CRM, and in this way, technology has revolutionized the traditional role of librarians in this field.

A New Partnership: The Business of Information

Ten years ago, there was likely to be some friction between a law firm's information technology (IT) department and its library, mainly due to a lack of communication on both parts. IT and the professionals who commanded the department were in high demand, as firms initiated e-mail, accounting and time billing systems, electric litigation support and much more back-off solutions. However, the emergence of CI or competitive intelligence has given the library much panache as well as center stage. As firms strive to stay competitive in a quickly changing industry, sophisticated strategy is necessary to make important business decisions whose ramifications could make or break the future of the firm. Such demand calls for scholarly granular information that can be used tactically for a firm's long-range strategic goals. The library will still be attached to technology 24/7 in order to insure that information is authoritative, timely information, however, this time IT will be seen as the conduit, not the ends in itself. Some libraries found that their needs were not fulfilled efficiently or on a timely basis, so they created a new librarian role, that of the electronic librarians to take care of their needs and act as a liaison to IT. Electronic librarians have their Masters in library science as well, but are extremely IT savvy and focus their energy on keeping law firm librarians tuned into all law firm technology initiatives, as well as supporting their department's technology needs, such as the integrated library system or library Web pages. An on-staff librarian who is electronic savvy and can act as Web master for the library's intranet is integral to making the library a more active player in the business of law that is conducted in large law firms. Trends such as the creation of CRM technology, increased competition in the legal realm, and the need for the in-depth analytical Fortune 500 sales and business information that enables a law firm to make decisions and handle client consulting have greatly expanded the role of the law firm librarian.

However, although librarians have always interacted with their firm's attorneys, in most cases they did not interact with the business of law. Librarians at our 620-attorney firm now have a partnership with the marketing and the IT departments; for each of us has important contributions to make to the firm's overall success. The marketing department is stellar at assisting attorneys with the sales aspects of law, while the IT department insures that the firm is technologically competitive. It has always been the role of the library to create and preserve the scholarship of law that is so vital to the service that a firm provides for its clients. The difference now is that in the past we always understand the scholarship of law, but typically not the business of law. Once a research request was completed, its impact was lost to the librarian who provided the background information used to pitch to a new client. However, these days the library is much more part of revenue generation. In our case, all three departments—marketing, IT, and the library—have now joined forces to make our law firm succeed. We are truly involved in "the business of information." Content is not just for scholarships and knowledge, but it is a product for sales. Research itself has evolved from traditional legal research to business research and now to CI or competitive intelligence. Not a data dump, CI has become a sophisticated succinct analysis that is used to a firm's competitive advantage either for cross selling to existing clients, courting new clients, and keeping track of their competition.

New Librarianship Duties: Contract and Copyright Management

One of the biggest changes to the role of law firm librarian pertains to the fact that we have gone from being strictly involved in content management to also handling contract management—and business contracts have changed a great deal over the past twenty years. First, there is a great deal more money involved in contracts these days. With all the mergers and acquisitions, information providers have three fold the information to sell to you. In actuality when you negotiate with West for Westlaw or Lexis/Nexis, you are purchasing the rights to practically ALL of their database information, only now it is all on one contract. Secondly, there are many new legal ramifications as far as copyrights and the contract itself. Concerns involve what information should be included and excluded in a contract, how long a contract lasts before it can be renegotiated and changed, and what information has been added and at what cost to the user? A needs assessment must be done to insure that you really need all the information that you are purchasing. This involves looking at usage reports using either Lookup Precisions or Onelog for those vendors that do not proceed such statistical information and coming to a conclusion yourself, before the negotiations begin. Before I sign a contract, I need to discuss the content with the staff and ask the lawyer practice heads whether they really need a particular resource. In-house counsel also needs to comb through each contract to make sure it is correct, because these contracts are binding. Vendors will hold you to a contract; therefore, it is essential to examine the small print. The contracts for the content are challenging, largely because information is not being purchased; it is being rented. The rate profoundly affects the business of law. Contract negotiation and management is a new science that is challenging and demanding for its exactness. Like technology, CI is the catalyst that takes librarians to the next step of firm administration, that of revenue production.

Additionally, it is critical for the librarian to ensure that everyone in the firm is aware of and complies with the copyright laws. That education process entails constant marketing—not just to the firm's lawyers, but to the copy center and mailroom as well. For example, we constantly receive calls from the copy center saying that someone in the firm just sent a book down to them, and they want it to be copied from cover to cover. Law firms have been sued for taking such actions, and we do not want our firm to turn up on *The American Lawyer's* front page. As a for-profit organization, we must comply with the copyright laws; there is no fair use in a commercial law firm setting. Therefore, we post signs and conduct orientation programs to go over these copyright issues with the firm's attorneys. We have a copyright page on our intranet, which is very sophisticated, granular, and to the point. Our inter-library loan policies go hand and hand with our copyright policies, and we strive to clarify what we can copy, what is fair use, and what we pass can out at a seminar.

Revenue Relationships

For years, law firm libraries have been considered firm overhead, and hefty overhead at that. The law library budget is in the top four or five budget items for a firm, with other key items including real estate, liability insurance, and associates salaries' costs. As the other costs are pretty much locked down, it is the library that is viewed by the administration and finance departments as the one area where cost savings can be realized. But the volatility of the legal industry, as well as the capricious cost increases mandated by an almost monopolistic publishers' field, make adhering to budget a Herculean feat. As the old adage goes, they own the cow and so they set the price of the milk. Prices continue to climb year after year, and libraries are forced to make cuts to realize budget. This is yet another responsibility for librarians today, for they must compare like information and make cuts without compromising the integrity of their collections. For years, clever librarians have tried to solve the cost issue by trying to collect enough from client-billed research to offset library administrative costs. Although this paradigm seems logical, I have yet to find a law library that has paid for itself. But there are other ways in which a library can showcase its worth to firm administration, and CI is the key player here. Teaming up with the marketing and sales endeavors of a firm and becoming part of the increase in profits plans is a win-win for the library. CI is an integral component to successful sales, recruiting, and the strategic decision making of the firm. For centuries, successful leaders have kept advisers close at hand to provide the information needed to fight battles, take over governments, and insure successful commerce. Ultimately, it is true that knowledge is power.

Marketing the Library's Services

It is increasingly essential for law firm librarians to market their services to the various departments within the firm. To that end, we give annual presentations to the other offices on any new resources that are available. Although these services are also promoted in the firm newsletter, we have found that such information is more readily absorbed when someone stands in front of you and says, in effect, "If you type this on your keyboard, you will get this answer." Indeed, we are always selling our resources by word of mouth, trying to leverage our services to the utmost; we may say, for example, "If you use this service, then maybe you would also like this service;" or "Do you know we also have this service that may help with this same area of the law?" There are many teachable moments in a law firm and they should be capitalized.

Marketing is a critical dimension of the role of today's law firm librarian, and it is necessary to realize that marketing does not simply mean sending out brochures. It should be an ongoing process; for example, if you are in an elevator with one of the firm's partners and you have their attention for six floors, it is important to seize the opportunity to say something positive about your team.

However, it can be difficult to make a law firm's financial and administration personnel understand that librarians can be businesspeople. Indeed, in order to earn the respect of those administrators, you must run your library like a shop, and that means that you cannot turn off its activities when you leave for the day.

An Expanding Role: New Training Requirements

The law firm librarian's role is increasingly a hybrid job of providing the right services to the right people at the right time for the right cost—which is easily said, and not so easily accomplished. The jurisdiction of law firm librarians has greatly expanded within recent years; for example, we have stepped into knowledge management along with IT, as well as sharing competitive intelligence services with the marketing department.

In order to meet the challenges of our expanding role, I often tell young librarians to take some business courses, such as an elementary class that is offered to M.B.A. students. It is enormously helpful for a librarian to be able to talk the talk of the other departments in his or her firm. Unfortunately, many librarians who have been in the same job for a number of years have a dated perception of their role. The next generation of law firm librarians needs to possess budget skills at a new level as well as management skills, because many firms have a four-generation workspace. I have worked with librarians who were retired and then came back to work from retirement at age seventy, and I have worked with librarians who have just graduated—and it takes significant savvy to be able to manage those different groups and have them work together as a solid, cohesive team.

Developing New Procedures and Practices

If you have always done something in a certain way, it is important to revisit that process, step back from it, and think about how you can improve it or look at it in a different way. If someone had told me five years ago that I needed to project manage contracts, I would have said, "I have my file folders and historical information at my fingertips; I do not need a tickler system to remind me about contract renewals." In reality, it turns out that I do.

Therefore, it is essential for every law firm librarian to look at their weaknesses, which in many cases may be budgetary. We are all being pressured to cut our budgets, while publishers are attached to a very dated paradigm involving enormous yearly costs increases, especially with respect to print media—and most law firms allocate only one percent of their revenues to their library budget. Therefore, law firm libraries are increasingly forced to cut both duplication of services as well information acquisition, and we have to walk a fine line between being fiscally responsible and compromising the law library's collection. Consequently, it is often a good idea to implement better budgetary, as well as contract management tickler systems.

Indeed, budgetary constraints have forced librarians to be more judicial in terms of how they pick their resources. You cannot be afraid of changing course and seeking out alternatives if it will mean a cost benefit to the firm, even though it may be all too easy to stay in the same rut when you have always done things in a certain way or used the same vendor. You need to embrace change; if you are afraid of it, you should not be in administration. There are librarians who have been researchers throughout their entire career and are extremely happy doing that, but if you are going to move into an administrative position at some level—e.g., a branch or assistant librarian—you cannot be afraid of the budget.

In order to effectively develop new procedures, it is critical that librarians closely assess new resources as well. When evaluating new technologies for a law firm's library, the main criteria to utilize include content; cost; ease of use; and support. The decision-making process for adopting new technologies or resources is often collaborative; for example, both the library and marketing departments at our firm analyzed possible CRM programs, and we each brought different views to the table. Our department's strength is based on the fact that not only do we know the content of a program, we also know its reliability, timeliness, and authority—and authority is everything in the legal world. You can Google information, but Google does not have a footnote that tells you where a certain source came from or when it was last updated—and attorneys are a citation population. Indeed, American law is built on precedent.

In order to be prepared for the new technologies that will soon be available to law firms such as ours, I try to build solid relationships with my top vendors, because I need to know what is coming down the pike so that I can plan ahead. Today's budget restraints are such that if you do not know that a product or service is coming out in the fourth quarter, you cannot purchase it or budget for it. In addition, contract information is being updated all the time. Ten years ago, you signed a contract and it remained unchanged until it was renegotiated at the end of the year. These days, however, when you sign a contract there may be an amendment to that contract a month later, and then another and another as additional content is added to adjust to attorneys' research needs.

Overcoming the Challenges and Difficulties that Face Law Firm Librarians Today

I believe that there are two main challenges facing today's law firm librarian. One is keeping the process of CI within our domain, while understanding that we need to develop a strong partnership with our firm's marketing department, based on the premise that everyone should do what they do best. But marketing is best at training and teaching attorneys how to do sales, and what we do best is finding the right information—and the right amount of information—to make the right decisions. A partnership between our departments provides a win-win for the firm. However, establishing such a relationship can be a challenge. Some marketing departments have a dim view of librarians, saying in effect, "Oh, anybody could Google that information," which we know is not true.

The other main challenge that we face involves contract management. The contract management process should be much like project management, in that it is helpful to use a tickler system to remind you on a monthly basis when certain contracts are coming up for renewal. Such a system also explains what you did last year, and which people are involved. Contract management is much more structured and task-oriented than it has ever been, largely because there are now so many more contracts to review.

However, meeting these challenges is becoming easier, now that law firm libraries are less isolated from back-office procedures. These days, we will look at what other departments are doing and emulate those processes as needed. For example, IT has used project management techniques to manage contracts for the past twenty years. Librarians must also follow the lead of their firm's financial department and implement monthly, rather than quarterly, reviews of their budgets. When your financial sheets come out, you must evaluate them much as an accountant would. Rather than simply saying, "Well, my budget went haywire," you need to consider the percentages of publishers' increases with respect to book versus online information; costs per attorney; the ratio of library staff to attorney staff; and the historical record of these figures. Such analysis helps to give your role greater validity.

Perhaps the greatest difficulty that today's law firm librarian faces pertains to constantly monitoring their firm's collection and managing the costs of that laborious process. For example, when making entries into our department's cost spreadsheet, we constantly need to compare our projected 2008 costs to our 2007 costs, including any percentage increases. Monitoring the costs of a law firm library is a full-time job, and there is a great deal of money involved; in addition, you need input from the firm's attorneys, which is always difficult to obtain because of their time schedules.

Another difficulty inherent in a law firm librarian's role involves the acceleration of intellectual property (IP) law; it is such an exact science that many librarians completely avoid it. It takes someone who is a good, seasoned researcher and has an intuitive feel for the entire multi-step IP process, including prior art history and prosecution, to make sure that research in this area is done properly. For example, you must have a thorough knowledge of many databases that you would not typically use on a frequent basis. Some small vendors may have that one nugget of information that needs to be part of your research trail.

Changing government relations or enforcement practices had also had a challenging impact on the role of librarianship, especially in terms of our budget. Every time a Sarbanes-Oxley-type of legislation is passed, the cost of managing a law firm library exhibits a domino effect. You have to purchase copies of new research; keep abreast of any changes in the regulations, and then update your database—and these costs often arise after you have already developed your annual budget.

Managing the Changing Landscape

In order to succeed as a law librarian in this changing landscape, it is important to first identify the changes you are facing, and then you need to be proactive, not reactive. For example, if it is evident that you have to be more fiscally responsible, you must strategize how you can set any needed changes in motion, and then list the tactics that you will use. You may, for instance, decide to increase your interaction with your vendors and ask to beta test any products that are coming out so that you can be on the cutting edge of new technology.

After you have identified needed changes, developed effective strategies and tactics, and initiated your changes, you then need to market what you have accomplished. Throughout the process you must be sure you have a handle on any contracts and that you are being proactive to people's needs, rather than waiting until there is a crisis.

Various outside resources have proven to be helpful in terms of managing the changing role of librarians within law firms, including the advisory boards of major vendors, as well as vendors' library relations groups. Networking is also useful as well as benchmarking against similar firms. I measure similarities by size of the firm and the number of office locations and have created a four-member benchmarking group. We meet by phone on a monthly basis to discuss a specific agenda and compare notes. This process has been useful, largely because we were all tired of having to read someone else's survey, for example, without knowing what their metrics were, or if the staff did competitive intelligence.

Ultimately, meeting the expanding role in the law firm and the challenge of breaking out of the traditional roles is one of the greatest difficulties librarians today face. As explored in this chapter, the role of the law firm librarian is constantly changing, and for that reason, this profession is not for the fainthearted. However, change is both inevitable and positive, and if you choose to embrace it, it is not so overwhelming. On a personal level, I try to come to work every day, thinking about how I can do what I did last year in a different way. That mindset goes back to my desire to be proactive as opposed to reactive, and it takes significant brainpower to outthink your firm's attorneys and prepare for the changes to come. I believe true success will come from breaking the paradigms and retooling ourselves as librarians. We must be adept at navigating change via new procedures and willing to embrace the techniques and technologies that will best enable us to do so.

Technology is the conduit in the new library associate's research skills; at the same time, you have to reach out to the people in your firm and teach them how to operate that technology. In many cases, spending ten minutes with someone in their office to walk them through a new process can be more productive than conducting four seminars on that topic. Interaction is extremely important. In addition, there may be up to four generations in a firm's workforce; therefore, management skills are important. We also need to have closer relationships with our vendors; it is essential to consult with them in order to get an advance understanding of what new types of technology are coming out.

Simply put, this is a profession that never sleeps, because it is part of the whole information explosion/revolution/quagmire that has taken place over the past ten to fifteen years. As the amount of information that librarians manage has continued to increase, the costs of managing that information have escalated as well; therefore, a law firm librarian has to be very bottom line oriented.

A native Texan, Linda Will received both her B.A. and M.L.S. from the University of Texas at Austin. A law librarian for more than thirty years, Ms. Will has worked at Vinson & Elkins (Houston), Holland and Knight (Tampa), Greenberg & Traurig (Miami), and is presently the director of information resources for Dorsey & Whitney (Minneapolis), where she also serves on the firm's KM, CRM, and intranet teams. Ms. Will is a past H.A.L.L. president and has served on several advisory boards to include: R.I.C.E., Information America, the Copyright Clearance Center, and the West Advisory Board. Ms. Will has spoken at workshops both national and abroad and has twice taught "Electronic Resources," at the University of Texas Graduate School for

Library Science. Presently serving on the editorial board for Thomson's Practice Innovations, *Ms. Will has been published in the ABA's* Law Practice Management, *the* National Law Journal, Legal Information Alert, Trends, *and most recently in ALM's* Legal Tech Newsletter. *In September 2008, Ms. Will was elected to be a Fellow in the College of Law Practice Management. She is the first librarian to be given such an honor.*

Active Librarianship in the Business-Oriented Law Firm

Laurie Daley

Librarian

Bullivant Houser Bailey

Introduction

Contrary to common stereotypes of libraries and librarians, work in the law firm library is not only exciting and challenging, but also frequently fast-paced. The law librarian is responsible for providing high-quality work from a variety of demanding and often high-pressure clientele including attorneys, their clients, and other staff members.

Challenges in Today's Law Library – Managing Expectations

Law librarians today take on the challenges of the business world. Successful law firms are run more and more like businesses. Attorneys are interested in firm revenue, profits per partner, and billing rates—and not as much about tradition and reputation. What impresses clients are low-cost, successful case resolutions, not the money spent on the firm's office decor.

Managing client perceptions and expectations is one of the most difficult aspects of my position as a law librarian, because these elements often go unspoken until something goes wrong, or escalates until someone is unhappy enough to speak out.

We have worked to educate attorneys about the added value of information professionals by emphasizing the quality of our work—providing in-depth, accurate information that goes beyond Google, using sources they have not thought about or do not know about. We also use National Library Week as a time for marketing ourselves. A couple of years ago we sent out a survey to establish how attorneys thought about the library and its services. The biggest response was that they wanted to know more about what constituted our services. That year, we distributed an oversized postcard that listed examples of our recent research projects.

Working with Attorneys – The Importance of Timing

Another key challenge is catching the attention of the attorneys to whom you want to reach out. Lawyers are extremely busy individuals, with a number of tasks they are working on at any given time. Whatever it is they are doing—be it managing various cases, attracting new clients, corresponding with current clients, or communicating with other departments who also want their attention—a good librarian will take the time and effort to figure out how to efficiently and effectively deliver a message. The same is true when dealing with firm management. The leaders of the firm have so many other items on their agenda, that sometimes problems you want fixed will not be addressed until they escalate.

These days, it is difficult to credit any single approach to marketing library services. We are more successful by using a variety of methods to appeal to as many people as possible—e-mail; short, targeted, issue-specific training to practice groups; one-on-one instruction; written research guides on our firm's Intranet; and of course, offering food as an incentive. In the majority of our offices, the library is less about being a "space" so we need to go where the attorneys are as well as anticipate where they will be.

Personally, time is the key element I take into consideration when evaluating anything that has to do with the library. Time is increasingly in short supply. For example, there is always an attorney who wants a research request done ASAP because he is meeting with a client in fifteen minutes. Also, tasks like evaluating new online catalog projects and available staffing resources can drain time all too easily. Working in the library rarely means getting to set your own timetables. Books pile up, invoices multiply, and e-mails need to be read. Keeping track of both physical and virtual worlds in the library requires a lot of time and energy.

Adding Value within the Firm

In today's law firm, libraries need to be seen as contributing value to the organization. In truth, they have always made a difference in the legal services that are offered by the firm, whether that is in the lower price clients pay because of negotiated discounts in online services, access to materials that are outside of the scope of attorneys, or even something as fundamental as setting up the system for checking out books so they can be found when they are not on the shelves. Many of these roles, though, are unfortunately invisible to the attorneys. All librarians in the setting of the law firm need to find ways of increasing the visibility of these internal processes if they are to maintain their place in the organization.

Library staff members are more important to the organization than the library itself. Obviously, it is necessary to have books and online services, but even more crucial are skilled professionals working to train people, answer questions, and actively solve problems. An online vendor is not going to go over to the local courthouse to find a law review that is older than its coverage; neither will it make an evaluation of which provider has the easiest access to dockets. And only a librarian will let you know there is a cheaper way to get the answer needed from another vendor.

Fiscal Concerns

Finance is another area where librarians need to manage expectations—that is, the expectations of our supervisors, our staff, and the firm management, as well as our own. Like many firms, mine has a diverse geographic attorney base. Six offices in four states may not seem overly eclectic; but it is certainly enough to increase the diversity of opinion and expectation. Cost recovery ratios, requests for new materials, and budget variances are all examples of financial issues that are addressed differently in our firm depending on the office.

Cost considerations are a greater factor than they used to be, and cost calculations have become more complex. Librarians are dealing with larger contracts with their vendors, with more materials, and in a wider variety of formats that offer more services—and it all comes at a much higher price. Again, other departments are unfortunately having the same dilemmas, and are fighting for a piece of the firm pie. This means there needs to be more time (which is in short supply, as I said earlier) spent compiling more information to support arguments for adding resources or additional staff.

At my first library, there was a "showcase" library, filled with many, many books, where all of the attorneys came to get their pictures taken. I remember a senior appellate attorney telling me that it was worth spending several hundred dollars on a set of books if it saved the client a million. The library was absolutely gorgeous—but this type of library is a rare sight anymore.

For the most part, the "showplace" attitude has been replaced with demonstrating to the client how fiscally responsible the firm is—how wisely it uses their fees and how few extra costs we add to the bills. Some firms are now building all attorney offices to the same size and dimension when they move into a new space, which cuts the cost of moving attorneys. Most attorneys also now meet with clients in conference rooms instead of their offices, so they are not impressing clients with snazzy views and fabulous furniture.

On this note, cost recovery is near the top of my list of concerns. The pressure to keep down costs comes not only from clients, but also from attorneys who have been using online services long enough that they have started to think clients should not be billed for them any more than they are billed for our electricity or rent. They believe it is reasonable for a client to assume that we have access to all case law information, and therefore it is reasonable to assume the client should not be billed for it. When an attorney does not believe online service charges should be billed, it is difficult for them to justify the costs to their clients. Initially, I discuss the firm's rationale for recovering the online research charges: we pay a lot of money to our online vendors and we want to recoup as much as we can in order to keep our expenses down. As the discussion has moved over time beyond individual attorneys to practice groups, some groups have elected to purchase flat-fee subscriptions for subject-specific services that will not be billed to clients to moderate use in the broader billable databases.

In the last couple of years, my budget has become more inelastic because of long-term contracts. My online subscriptions budget is dominated by our Westlaw and Lexis contracts, and I tie the rest of the annual increases to the terms stated in those contracts. The budget for most of the print materials is going the same way. Last spring I signed a LMA with Thomson West and now the annual percentage increase is tied to my budget. There is definitely a need to educate the firm's administration about how library budgets are different from budgets in other departments. Our accounting department gives a suggested increase at the beginning of the budget process, and I have been significantly outside of the guidelines for the last two to three years. However, I document all of my contracts and send copies to our CFO, as well as use spreadsheets to track increases, and the budget gets approved. In the increasingly small area that lies outside of our contracts, it is important to involve attorneys in decision making for weeding materials as well as making new purchases. Costs have to be monitored constantly.

Licensing Concerns

Contracts have become increasingly complex. Because of acquisitions, there are fewer vendors in the marketplace, but the negotiation process can take months in examining options and arriving at a compromise. Privacy issues, regarding how we get background information and how we use it, are another concern. Librarians have to be careful in ensuring their patrons are not using sensitive information without the correct legal purposes, because we sign contracts that require these motives. Also, privacy is required in contract negotiations by signing non-disclosure agreements.

On my part, this has translated into more time working with vendors or reviewing our contracts, usage reports, and more time spent scrutinizing invoices. I personally wish that library school, at the time I was attending, had discussed how important online resources would be in our professional lives. There is an incredible amount of money spent investing online resources, and librarians have to invest their time in fitting them to the needs of their organization.

Technology

Technology continues to change research methodologies, or at least peoples' perception of change itself. Looking back ten to fifteen years ago, there was a lot of discussion (which still continues) about how librarians need to adapt to changes in technology, how people are working and communicating with new tools, and how it affects the practice of law. There is a constant need for continuing education for librarians. I tell attorneys that they can't assume they use a product well because they learned it in law school, and the same is true for us. Keeping up to date by reading professional literature and attending seminars and webinars is essential for maintaining relevancy in the law firm. We're all looking for competitive advantages, and successfully adapting technology to a new service, product, or even a cost savings makes the library look good to the firm administration and the firm look good to clients.

It is hard to add time for evaluating new products and technologies into an already full day, week, or month. Sometimes, like a new docket service, it just happens to be the right call at the right time at the right price.

Sometimes, the call comes from someone in another department who has seen a product they think would be helpful for research. I find that I am more reluctant to commit time to evaluate new products than I used to be, so I need to see a clear research application pretty quickly. I also quickly assess the likelihood and ease of use in my firm—if it's not useful for our attorneys and their workflow then it's a waste of time and money. I'm not crazy about committing my time, and even less so about theirs.

Responding to These Challenges – the Librarian's Dynamic Role

In order to meet these challenges successfully, many librarians have been given broader responsibilities within their organizations. In some firms, librarians manage other departments like records and conflict checking. In others, they direct functional areas like knowledge management or the corporate intranet. Many have librarians assigned to work with individual practice groups.

I generally judge my level of job satisfaction in terms of my performance in addressing challenges. I feel most pleased having contributed to a difficult project, or even just having helped out with a complex research question. When I first started in my current position, I would hold up my performance to my predecessor—if I was not doing better (according to my own standards, of course), then I would try to figure out how to improve for the next time around.

Documentation and reports are always useful in tracking important data I want to keep an eye on, such as best practices, or how librarians are doing in accomplishing goals. There is no point, for example, in keeping track of inter-library loans if you cannot demonstrate how these support the value of the library in the larger organization. On the other hand, this data could be used to support an argument for hiring more staff to support the firm's increase in products liability litigation. Statistics can be extremely useful, but you need to apply serious analysis to the application, eventual usefulness, and presentation to decision makers.

Communication and Partnering

Luckily, the bedrock of librarianship is customer service and attention to detail, both of which serve the library staff and their patrons well. Communication is essential in working through challenges, be they with firm management, attorneys, or library staff. With more avenues for communication, though, it is important to discern which option is the best medium for the situation at hand.

Librarians make good partners, which is beneficial to a law firm's success. As other departments have risen in prominence—information technology, client services, and now professional development—librarians have resources and skills to share. We work with all of these departments to improve our services and theirs for the greater good of the organization, and to increase our own visibility and skills. It is a win-win situation. Sometimes it means sharing staff and splitting costs. A number of the larger projects in our firm have applications across departments. When we recently purchased a new research tool, marketing paid for half and the library paid for half. The other library staff member works half time in the library and half time on the IT help desk. While I would much rather have her as another full-time librarian, I appreciate her practical computer and training skills.

As a solo librarian, colleagues outside of the firm have been invaluable. Whether it is for practical advice, locating a missing treatise, or just providing an understanding ear for venting frustration, it is wonderful to be the beneficiary of our service profession. Professional associations like AALL or SLA provide information about the broader issues, and I have been lucky enough to go to several annual conventions. Each year there has been at least two or three sessions that made me seriously re-evaluate and change something about what, how, or why I have been providing a service.

Bringing Traditional Skills to Address New Challenges

The most important skill that librarians need to thrive in their environments is still the traditional value of great customer service. Also, problem solvers do well with the challenges that present themselves, which is certainly a necessary capability in today's library. Librarians reliably pay attention to details, which is a habit that has served them well in transitioning to new services and products—whether that is rolling out a new library catalog that now includes pictures of books and links to tables of contents, or compiling expert witness materials into Web-based databases. Librarians today succeed by utilizing the task mastery and values they acquired during the beginning of their careers, and playing these qualities to their strengths.

It is to librarians' advantage to promote different services and products to their patrons as technologies change. Librarians are excellent opportunists as well as problem solvers. I think the importance of customer service to us leads us to see where we can apply technological solutions to the best advantage of our organizations. Successful librarians are always looking for ways to improve their departments, and luckily, most librarians have become good at figuring out where things potentially go wrong before their attorneys do.

At a very basic level, I do not think the objectives and goals of librarians have changed much in the last few years. I believe successful librarians have implemented many of the traditional skills of librarianship in order to manage the changes in their organizations. While drawing on tradition is not a new practice, of course, I do think librarians now address this support in more targeted approaches, and with a clearer focus as to how their processes and projects promote the goals and direction of the firm.

Laurie Daley has been a librarian at Bullivant Houser Bailey since 2003. Previously, she was a librarian at Lane Powell from 1999 to 2003. Ms. Daley received her B.A. from the University of Oregon and her M.L.S. from Syracuse University.

Dedication: *To Annetta Lawson, colleague and friend extraordinaire; and Paul Daley, supportive husband.*

Law Firm Librarianship: Moving Toward Harnessing Knowledge in a Changing Informational Landscape

Elaine M. Egan
Legal Information Manager
Mayer Brown LLP

Introduction – A Changing Role

Librarians historically acted as information seekers, recorders, and keepers. Generally, they were highly educated in a specific discipline and academically trained. Both public and academic institutions typically employed those who are practiced in areas rich in research and functioned in identifiable roles within the walls of the library. The "old-school" librarian in the private sector in many ways was the maintainer of a collection, with a skill for research. The consensus today is the professional M.L.S. or M.L.I.S. is the foundation for all librarians practicing in the public, academic, and private sector organizations.

Typically, law librarians receive specific training as part of their M.L.S./M.L.I.S. curriculum; this includes legal citation research, legal research, and in some instances a focus on legal cataloguing.

In specific areas of law librarianship, a J.D. (Juris Doctorate) is required; those positions typically fall in the federal court system and law school libraries. In fact, the American Bar Association requires all approved law schools should have a library director with a J.D. This role in most circumstances is also considered a faculty appointment and thus a tenured-track position.

Law firms tend to hire librarians without J.D.s, but for the most part require the M.L.S./M.L.I.S. The true test of skill in a law firm is that the core competencies for the specific need such as research are met. There is some discussion in the profession that the J.D. may be considered undesirable in the law firm environment for a number of reasons, one of which may be that a librarian with a J.D. may be encouraged to make legal determinations.

There are currently eight U.S. universities with joint M.L.S./J.D. programs. Some debate that the addition of a J.D. will become the required norm in both law firms as well as academic settings. Most scholars take a view that specialization in a field will become more valuable over time, for instance someone skilled in a particular area of law or language. However, one truism in librarianship exists—that is, the ability to meet the challenges of a changing information landscape.

The ever-evolving information needs of each generation have resulted in the revaluing of the information professional/librarian as one who steers us down the *information highway*. The last ten years of expansive growth in information access and content has compelled librarians to reinvent their roles. What does this cosmic shift signify? The public's adapting to the *information age* demands trained information professionals/librarians who are able to effectively sift through and organize vast quantities of information rapidly. The Internet and supporting technologies are obviously responsible for much of this explosion. Yet, while information can be accessed faster than what was imaginable only a decade ago, librarians now must face the difficult issue of *source credibility* accompanied by *information overload*.

As in any profession dealing with tested and substantive knowledge, law firms experience source credibility and information overload in abundance. Lawyers, just as the general population, assume much of the information they obtain via the Internet is a reliable true source. Qualifying and determining credibility has added a new dimension to supporting valid research. James Wales, founder of Wikipedia, recently issued a statement calling upon librarians to become more involved in dealing with information from the Internet. "The job of the librarian is about highlighting the weaknesses and strengths of information."[1] This call for information professionals to engage in the effective harnessing of expert information and influencing search strategy would have a powerful effect on driving up the standard of information deemed worthy of research inclusion. This issued has longed been identified among librarians for some time—that not all pieces of information grabbed from the online universe are credible or useable. Anyone can post content on the Web, and the lack of built-in filters means a wide range of content resides side by side and is retrieved from the same access point. The limited standardized process for vetting and evaluating information leaves the researcher in a *buyer beware* scenario.

Within the legal profession, the credibility issue spawned the fee-based Legal Information Content Universe. Standard print publishing sources utilized in the practice of law quickly realized the potential of delivery

---

[1] Mark Chillingworth, Information World Review, *Wales Summons Librarians to Help improve Wikipedia* http://www.linuxinsider.com/story/Wales-Summons-Librarians-to-Helps-Improve-Wikipedia-61213.html?welcome=1204562022 (Jan 15, 2008).

through electronic access via software and now, of course, the Internet. This industry has flourished by instilling confidence in source credibility and authorship, allowing lawyers to manage their practice through their laptop, PDA, or desktop. This working model developed dedicated believers in fast, reliable content, and as we know, not all content is created equal.

Therefore, what should a law librarian consider when evaluating content on the Internet? Librarians skilled at evaluating print sources have been able to transfer this skill to the electronic software and World Wide Web. The following are just basic guidelines a librarian would use to evaluate most sources including web-based content.

1. Accuracy: What is it?
2. Authority: Who is it?
3. Objectivity: How is it?
4. Currency: When is it?

Information overload in a law firm as a result of the surge of necessary *knowledge or know-how* required for the practice of law has elevated the law firm librarians off the endangered species list to more expanded critical role in a firm. Lawyers at their core are power users of information. Law firms gather, create, receive, and organize knowledge. Most law firms were not engaged in the initial phases of technologically harnessing internal intellectual property. However, the new global business model of client support, collectively sharing and certifying your work product is key to realizing a law firm's full potential and that of their most valuable asset, *attorney capital*. Harnessing knowledge has law firms strategizing on how best a firm can leverage content *"within"* (the firm work product) and leverage content *"without"* (fee-based source content). The challenge in this environment is to limit information overload. By identifying the internally and externally available knowledge effectively, the information professional selects sources that separate rich content from shear volume and targets the key recipients. Leading firms have really taken the *knowledge management/know-how management* concept to a level that is global in scope while others have been committed to supporting these initiatives at a basic functional document level. At issue on both sides of the KM solution is the all-important problem of content credibility. The notion that if you use your own work product along with credible fee-based content, then some filtering, limiting overload and assuring credibility is achieving the valuable KM objective.

Librarians that migrate toward knowledge management in its various incarnations have become organizational *center of influence*. The law firm librarian is a key professional prepared for the assessment of content credibility, source identification, users' skills, and user behavioral trends. KM trends and the vision for each firm are typically identified as an organized, institutional approach to delivering the *critical information* to *key people* at the *right time*. The results are developing effective work habits; enhancing competitiveness; reaching fiscal objectives; and limiting exposure to risk. Since librarians are a central supporting focus of this new paradigm, their sphere of influence has entrenched them in the law firm corporate structure and they are a featured component of the law firm's strategic plan.

Responding to Changes in Law Library Technologies

What drives investment in technology? The increasingly complex global economic environment drives innovation, speed, and flexible working models. Law firms that have strategized by combining their practices and knowledge assets into a seamless delivery chain that connects employees and their clients have accelerated in the global environment. These firms, make use of CMS portals, shared workspaces, e rooms, IM, wikis, blogs, and RSS. The pace of a law firm can be both fast and unpredictable; when you are committed to maintaining new working models and technologies, they need to be supported on a regular basis. This commitment requires financial dedication, time, and skilled individuals: *content evaluators* (librarians); *content specialist* (attorneys) and *delivery specialists* (IT).

The librarian is therefore a strengthening force for KM solutions. By identifying the need to evaluate content as well as to shift "user" cultural behavior, librarians typically start with the vital collaborative relationship with a lawyer or practice area. This collaborative relationship is comprised of many elements from supporting specific electronic content needs, training, current awareness dissemination, content delivery mechanisms, client outreach, and uniquely supporting internal blogs and wikis (wikis *allow editing for multiple participant blogs or community sites*). Building the shared community of knowledge has been common for legal practice groups for years. This was previously a *one-on-one* "drop-in" session, moving quickly to e-mail communication and now the blog. If a firm has multiple offices across borders, or even across oceans, blogging is an excellent way to share information and further develop a team approach within a company. Unlike e-mail, the blog has a personal feel to it and gives a sense of an open forum rather than e-mail user group or a private e-mail communication.

Dynamic blogs should be timely and have frequent daily postings featuring a leading case or legal issue within your practice group. The blog should encourage sharing recent changes in the law, address specific client solutions and be highly focused on a niche or specific practice area. The internal blog establishes the author as reliable and builds credibility among the blog practice area "community." Though a rather simple solution, there are some who theorize that the blog is a potential Knowledge Management tool. The concept being that this simple inexpensive sharing device can in some instances become more successful than expensive KM systems. Librarians uniquely support internal blogs by supplying RSS Newsfeed opportunities, posting leading cases and delivering current awareness content solutions that reflect the user cultural trends. Library blogs serve the internal librarian network through a shared research experience, evaluation of sources, and the development of the librarian community within the firm focused on sharing knowledge via traditional and technological platforms.

KM "search training," e-rooms, and portals that facilitate the sharing of information among attorneys and clients are phenomena that have become more prevalent and are changing rapidly. Librarians teaming with Information Technology Departments develop solutions that control the flow of vital information and free attorneys to focus on collaboration, research, and results. The fast delivery of information is a vital element in law firm knowledge management, and librarians today are faced with finding methods to ensure that key content is reaching key individuals.

As in most professions, librarians need to embrace and leverage technology solutions. Law firms tend to respond to technology solutions based on client needs and requests. As the next generation of attorneys adapts to the global technology enterprise so will the training and academic foundations of future librarians.

Key Legal Issues

Librarians are faced with legal issues in traditional adherence to copyright, licensing agreements, client confidentiality, user access and privacy, but with technology front and center. At root, a fundamental value that a free society offers is equal access to information and basic tools. These tools make certain assumptions and exploit technology to best serve the society.

Progressive technologies have posed new issues concerning the copying, downloading, and transmittal of digital works distributed via the Internet. The implications of unauthorized use of these works extend beyond what was originally intended. New legislation by states, the federal government, and international organizations will likely grow in influence in the near term.

Licensing agreements, a rarity several years ago, is now a primary focus in the sale of journals, newspapers, newsletters, and in law firms, the electronic practice area treatises. This method of access allows for multiple users to have simultaneous access to the same service or publication. In some instances licenses are restricted to one user at a time as though the work or journal were actually physically on a shelf and *"checked out"* to a user while another waits their turn. This has become less popular over time since publishers can roll up multiple user licenses at a premium and librarians tend to want unlimited access for their library patrons.

Restricting access to material in the public arena or Internet within a private or corporate institution can be imposed "upstream" of transmittal and "downstream" by filtering of sources deemed *nonbusiness* in relevance more realistically than in a public institution. The constitutional elements of access are typically tested in the public library or public academic system. Leading cases that discuss censorship through restricting access as well as evaluating risks to minors is always a debate between the courts, the public, and the library profession.

Getting Attorneys Involved

The primary element of success in any law firm initiative is the support of attorneys. It is critical to include attorneys when developing new strategies and solutions. A library director should develop a strategic plan and assign a planning committee, one that includes not only key library personnel, technology engineers, executive decision makers, but more importantly, attorneys. It isn't good enough for the right decision to be made and then fail to get the right people behind it. Identifying solutions, raising productivity levels and profitability spark collaboration and support from the attorney sphere of influence.

Financial Strategies

Part of strategic planning also involves financial strategies; over the last several years, law firm libraries have been tooling budgets and forecasting expenditures. As a financial plan is developed, librarians need to first consider the goals of the firm. Director librarians have to project budgets that include multi-year agreements and be knowledgeable enough to make the right changes in agreements, and to create budgets that contain costs. One of the most frequent complaints about financial planning is that a number is now replacing value.

Software and Web-based products are in the marketplace that allow librarians to monitor all electronic use within their organization. These tools identify what sources are being leveraged and are cost effective, versus those that are used only infrequently and out of line financially with their in-house value. These programs feature metrics such as cost per minute and attorney use, and help to establish benchmarks year over year or the term of the license.

Line by line and month by month accountability is more important than ever. This is challenging because of certain misperceptions related to electronic access in relation to the cost of print. Attorneys often believe, wrongly, that electronic sources ought to be less expensive. These collection-balancing issues deal with print versus electronic sources and the generational training gaps that place these mediums in conflict. Print will never be completely phased out, therefore librarians are always struggling to support two levels of access.

Transitioning From Print to Electronic Information

Balancing print medium and electronic sources is a struggle facing most libraries and law firms are no exception. The advent of web-based and electronic information has perpetuated the print verses electronic debate.

This debate is actually complex. Rapid technology advancement as we know it presents the sense that all material is available electronically. Quite the contrary.

The initial transition from print to electronic in law firms began in 1970 with Mead Data Central (MDC), a division of the Mead Corporation. MDC, in conjunction with the Ohio State Bar, launched a database through a dedicated computer that offered full text searching of Ohio and New York State cases. In 1980, Lexis offered Nexis a searchable database of news articles—hence, the present branding LexisNexis. In 1975, West Publishing, the premier legal reporter publisher that developed the headnote search and digest feature, launched Westlaw. Westlaw offered a database also through a dedicated computer for full-text searching of federal cases and selected state reporters. These two electronic publishers through various corporate buyouts, acquisitions, and restructurings continue to offer the lion share of electronic legal and non-legal material utilized in the law firms, law schools, and the court system. LexisNexis is part of the Anglo-Dutch publisher Reed Elsevier and Westlaw is part of West, a Thomson Reuters business.

Once this method of case law searching took root, the next natural progression for sources available through the electronic medium grew. Electronic treatises, area of law multi-volume services, newsletters, forms, practice tools, statutes, and rules have become the norm. However, traditional print research is not lost entirely. There are many valuable sources still unavailable electronically—not to mention historic material yet to be digitized. There are those practice professionals and scholars who feel that a serious researcher should be trained and skilled using print material and this skill enables one to be a more efficient electronic researcher.

Cross-Generational Training

Of all the themes that law librarians contend with, one that is vital and often overlooked is cross-generational teaching. A law firm is made up of a structured hierarchy consisting of partners, associates, counsel, paralegals, administrative staff, and executive staff. Within the partner pool there is often a wide range of those who have practiced for thirty-five years and the first year associate. There are always significant learning styles among individuals, but factoring in the added component of the generation creates complexities in achieving unified training objectives. Organizations tend to focus on multigenerational learning groups whose teaching styles do not benefit the "learner." Firms may recognize that attorneys should be grouped in training sessions while paralegals in other sessions based on their *need to know*, but within those groups learning can be vastly different.

There are a few strategies that can aid in reaching your multi-generational law firm. Start by identifying the generation: Nexters/Millenials, Generation Xers, Baby Boomers, and Veterans. Each of these generations receive and process information differently. Some are more apt to work in groups, while others learn best one on one. Approaching how the library can work with each group not only builds skill sets among attorneys but also builds the relationship between the attorney patron and library.

Conclusion: Build Relationships to Leverage Support Among Peers

It is absolutely crucial that librarians not only build attorney support but develop it with peer directors and managers within their organization. To stand alone and isolated in an organization leaves a department with a lack of focus and is at risk of being viewed as not valuable to the firm. Learning from peers who have skill sets they are willing to share elevates knowledge within your organization and promotes in-house education and training, while at the same time fostering a more general sense of inter-organizational connectivity. Meeting with finance people increases knowledge for developing fiscal strategies; sitting down regularly with the IT team helps identify content delivery options and enhancements; meeting with an HR manager enforces best practices in staffing mentoring and management. Partnering with peer managers and directors within your own organization is an invaluable skill—and there is almost nothing more important than being an active member of your law firm's community.

The Scope of Librarianship Today

There are a number of universal goals that librarians can reach for, but particular libraries also need to focus on their own specific goals. One universal goal is to deliver the best product to your user—the firm you work for on behalf of their client—and in the most cost-efficient way possible.

Another goal is to elevate the perception of what librarians and libraries offer to their firms in terms of productivity and profitability. Librarians should make efforts to communicate that their position is not a *center of expense* but a *center of value*. This is accomplished by tying library service to a valuable revenue stream; while you are not directly responsible for bringing in clients or dollars, the idea is that the library is part of the success of the revenue stream. The product you deliver and its credibility will promote this mission. If information services is only considered an expense within the firm, then the potential to achieve information goals is seriously constricted.

The jurisdiction of librarians has expanded in certain areas over the past five to six years. Some firms have had very highly skilled researchers move into corporate practices in the marketing and competitive intelligence function. There are competitive intelligence researchers/librarians who align themselves with a practice area strategist or who have moved into a marketing and business development practice.

Knowledge management officers can also rise from a library. Their efficiencies in information architecture are in many ways the most effective way to get that program initiated.

Librarians increasingly play roles as firm administrators. This has sparked a new round of professional development needs that involve mastering metrics, developing productivity measures, reviewing budgets as line items as well as reviewing budgets in terms of firm initiatives, presenting, negotiating contracts, and identifying staffing needs. In line with all of this, librarians need to define what they want or need to excel in these roles. Having been bombarded by so many changes, librarians have expanded in areas where there was formerly an in-house expert. Stretching professionally by participating in professional associations; American Libraries Association (AALL); Special Libraries Association (SLA); International Association of Law Libraries (IALL); and Knowledge Management Professional Society (KMPro) provide support and learning opportunities.

There are countless other national and regional forums on technology, knowledge management solutions, and global strategic planning of information run by management conference boards and companies like the Ark Group.

Librarians are generally solution driven personalities that thrive on new challenges and opportunities to support knowledge. Channeling this strength in an information age is not new to this profession; information growth has been spawned at various points over the centuries. Librarians and scholars have always found ways to respond to these changes and the age of information technology is no exception.

Elaine M. Egan is the legal information manager for Mayer Brown LLP in New York. She is a board member of the local AALL chapter: Law Library Association of Greater New York (LLAGNY), a member of the American Association of Law Libraries, the Special Library Association, and the International Association of Law Libraries. Ms. Egan is an alumni member of the Thomson West Advisory Board.

She received her M.L.S. from St. John's University along with her B.S. in journalism and communications.

The Law Firm Librarian and the Business of Law

Lynn Connor Merring
Manager, Library, Records, and Docket
Stradling Yocca Carlson & Rauth

I am the second librarian who has served at our one hundred attorney law firm, and I have recently started my ninth year at the firm. My predecessor was here for ten years; she had been the firm's Lexis account rep and did not have a Master of Library Science (M.L.S.) degree. The role of librarian is changing at our firm, partly because of my input and my background. I have both an M.L.S. and a Juris Doctor (J.D.) degree and considerably more experience than my predecessor; therefore, I bring a much wider view to the role.

There has also been an increasing emphasis in recent years on the use of technology to improve library efficiency and effectiveness, and a wider view of the value of information to the firm. Materials that previously were only available in hardcopy are now purchased in electronic format instead, so they can be accessed by attorneys in all five offices, not just by those with access to the library. Additionally, the librarian's job at our firm has been expanded to include records and docketing. Client files are no longer regarded as just papers that have to be filed but instead recognized for the wealth of information contained in them and now made readily accessible to the attorneys for the benefit of our clients.

In the past the library was more reactive; now we are very proactive. I review a wide variety of news and legal publications every day so I can alert the attorneys to information of interest to them or their clients. I actively seek (and receive) information on the firm's business plans so that I can be prepared for expansion, whether in terms of the number of attorneys or offices or in new practice areas.

Responding to Current Trends

I think the expansion of management of all forms of information is one of the biggest trends affecting the law firm librarian profession these days. Putting the records department under my control, for example, changed this department from being just a storage function to a real risk management tool. I see value in the documents, not just papers to be stored and retrieved. Because I have a J.D., I am very much aware of risk management issues arising from the way the documents are handled, retained, or destroyed.

The library now does a lot of outreach to other departments, including marketing, billing, and IT. Just as I keep the attorneys abreast of news and current developments, I do the same for our administrative departments. I provide research services to the marketing department and to attorneys who are gathering information to take to marketing.

Consequently, I believe that the single most important skill for today's law firm librarian is the ability to run the library as a business. A law firm is just that—a business. Therefore, the library must function to support that business—i.e., to improve the bottom line. If it cannot do that, it should not exist. Any procedures that do not add to the bottom line must be changed, and just because we have always done something does not mean that we must always do it. If the firm has ALWAYS subscribed to certain loose-leaf services but now those services can be provided at a lower cost and in a more useful format through online subscriptions, that change should be made and the training required to support the transition being organized and delivered.

Hard copy publication costs are skyrocketing, and while publishers need to be more reasonable in pricing, the law firm librarian must do their part to help their firm meet this financial challenge and others. For example, when evaluating new technologies (such as switching from hard copy to electronic or from CD-ROM to Internet access), I always look to the bottom line—i.e., how will this technology make me or my lawyers more effective or efficient? What is the return on investment (ROI)?

I am not big on formal procedures; I have always had fairly small staffs. I always look for things that could be done differently, better—or not at all; then I look for ways to address that concern. My firm does not have a library budget; I am expected to spend what I need in order to do what needs to be done, and to negotiate the best deals possible. That enables me to be very flexible and requires that I be very diligent about watching the bottom line.

Primary Objectives and Goals of the Librarian: An Expanding Role

Indeed, I believe that the primary objectives and goals of the law firm librarian are to make the firm more efficient, effective, and successful. These objectives are primarily driven by the bottom line; client demands;

and changes in our clients' industries. Perhaps the most challenging aspect of this role is balancing the needs and the dollars. The lawyers AND the clients need to understand the value of what we are asking them to pay for—why it is in their best interests, for example, to use online research instead of books in some situations.

The jurisdiction of librarians within a law firm has greatly expanded in recent years—in many cases because librarians have been banging on the "walls" of their libraries and demanding to expand. For example, I now manage our firm's records department because the firm sees value in a manager who understands information and its use, as well as its organization. They also appreciate that I have a law degree and therefore understand the risk management side of things. They can trust me to understand the law behind retention schedules and the need for destruction of records. That recognition allowed me to further expand our services into the development of a docketing department, which tracks all litigation and the deadlines involved in each matter.

I believe that it is essential for librarians to respond to any new organizational challenges that are presented. In addition, you need to look for information needs that are under or not served, and jump into action. For example, one of the tasks that I offered to assume early on was to take all the phone calls reception could not figure out what to do with. I am in a unique position to have an overview of the firm, as well as access to the records department database; therefore, I am the logical person to handle such calls. This initiative quickly established me as a "can-do" person who was willing to take on any job that would benefit the firm.

Looking ahead, I believe that new types of managerial training need to be in place for the next generation of law firm librarians, including more emphasis on the business of information. These training requirements differ greatly from those that existed in the past; I do not remember ever talking about the business side of the equation in school. As information has become more important, so has the ability to organize and manage it. Librarians at many law firms are moving into record and docket management, as I have done, as well as competitive intelligence, and even marketing.

Meeting Challenges

One of the most difficult challenges of being a law firm librarian can be getting the firm's new attorneys to understand that asking for help in the library is a good thing, not a sign of weakness. There is often a fear among new attorneys that they will be perceived as not being able to cut it if they ask for library assistance; when in fact, the firm expects them to take advantage of the librarian in order to become more effective and efficient.

Another challenge for today's law firm librarians involves operating the library as a business. Firms do not have libraries because they are noble; a law firm library must add to the bottom line. It can be difficult to overcome this challenge because we are, for the most part, an overhead expense. However, if we go out and aggressively market our skills to the entire firm, and become part of the fabric of both managing the business and servicing its clients, we cannot help but be successful. In library school (at least back in the dark ages when I was in school) there was a lot of emphasis on the notion that libraries are inherently good and therefore deserve support. Maybe that works for public libraries but in law firms (or any business) they deserve support ONLY so long as they add to the entity's bottom line. You know that you have achieved this goal when the powers that be (whether managing partners or other administrators) start seeking you out to help solve problems or address new challenges.

On a personal level, my ability to prove my worth to the firm stems from assignments such as being allowed to take over the records department and develop a formal, centralized docketing department. My job has stayed interesting to me because I have been allowed to grow in the job. And I have been allowed to grow because I have demonstrated both my professional abilities AND my understanding of the firm's business needs and goals.

Librarians as Diplomats and Marketers

Today's librarians must acquire two important skills in order to become successful at law firm librarianship—diplomacy and marketing. A law firm is a business; therefore, you need diplomacy in order to balance the egos of lawyers against the needs of the organization as a whole. Marketing is an important way to make the librarian and the library more visible and valuable—and thereby enhance the value of the firm as a whole.

Indeed, today's librarians are often expected to assist in marketing the services of the firm's library—and there are as many ways to do this as there are librarians. A librarian's marketing function is largely dependent on the librarian's skills and interests, and on the firm's culture. For example, the attorneys at my firm love the fact that I send out e-mails with valuable bits of news (cases of interest, economic developments in the local community, etc.). I do not do it regularly—only when I see something they need to know. However, the attorneys know that they can count on me to be reading the print and electronic sources that are most important to them, and to keep them posted. In addition, when they see an e-mail from me they know that it will be short and to the point, so they read it.

It is important for law firm librarians to effectively communicate their library's services, because we do not function in a vacuum. If no one knows who you are and what you are doing, are you really doing anything of value? When developing communication techniques, you need to assess your users and target their preferred style. For example, I use a lot of brief e-mails in order to transmit general information; I always have a sound bite ready for an elevator conversation; and I often hand deliver material to remind people who I am. I then ask them how I can improve my service.

Communication or marketing mistakes can best be avoided if you do focus on what YOU want to tell or how YOU want to tell it. Rather, it is important to focus on what THEY need to know, and how THEY prefer to find out that information.

The best way to obtain these important diplomacy and marketing skills is to always keep your eyes and ears open. It is important to attend American Association of Law Libraries (AALL) and other conferences; talk with the other administrators at your firm and others; and read not just professional publications, but business material as well. One of the most beneficial periods of my career was managing a library for GTE. I was able to take advantage of their in-house business training, and I got an incredible non-library business education. I learned a lot about managing employees, getting people to buy into new programs, and how to determine when it's time to grab the reins and lead—even if you are not in the "leadership" position on the organization chart.

Final Thoughts

My whole career as a law firm librarian is proactive. I am more aggressive these days in terms of taking a business approach to this position, and I think more librarians are doing the same. Hopefully, I can solve many problems before they become really problematic; therefore, I think the firm gets considerably more bang for my salary buck than they did with respect to the librarian role in previous years.

Lynn Connor Merring is the library, records, and docket manager at Stradling Yocca Carlson & Rauth. She has twenty-eight years experience managing law libraries in courts, corporations, and law firms. She has a B.A. in English, religion, and philosophy from Mary Washington College, her M.L.S. from Indiana University, and her J.D. from Indiana University.

Dedication: *To Alma Koelsch, who made me want to be a librarian, my parents who helped be become one, and my husband who has almost as many degrees as I do.*

Law Librarianship, Then and Now

Cindy Adams

Associate Director of Library Services

McKenna Long & Aldridge LLP

Introduction

In 1981 as I was studying for my Master's degree, one of my teachers at Emory University was the first professional law firm librarian in Atlanta. At that time, there were about a dozen professional librarians in Atlanta firms. Since then, I watched firms of all sizes gradually begin to hire people for the job, and the profession of the law librarian has grown and expanded since. The position flourished because attorneys perceived the value of having a professional on staff to organize print materials and deliver necessary information. Recently, the role of the law librarian has broadened from solely legal research into the realm of the business and competitive intelligence research. When I began my career, most of the day was spent pulling cases, statutes, and analysis materials. Now law librarians rarely perform substantive legal research anymore—what we do generally relates more to industry research, business information, and competitive intelligence.

Technology clearly has played a role in this evolution, and has also made the profession of law librarianship more difficult and complex. It affects collection development, library budgeting, departmental interactions, and most of all, research. The view persists that everything is on the Internet, and is free. As publication costs grow in excess of 10 percent each year, educating firm management about the necessity of high quality information continues to be a struggle.

Years ago, collection development was relatively simple. If you wanted to know if a particular treatise was being used, you might employ the "rubber band test." If there was a publication you were considering taking out of your collection, you would put a rubber band around it—if somebody used the book, they would take the rubber band off and never put it back; this way you knew whether certain books were or were not being used. As for different formats, there was only print. Now the decision is not only should we purchase an item, but also should it be print, electronic, online, or accessed through a third-party vendor.

Today, with electronic resources, it is almost impossible to know what is useful to attorneys unless you also purchase software that tracks usage. Electronic versions of print products are almost always more expensive than their print counterparts. Without tracking software, a library could be paying large sums of money for products which are not being used. Because of developments like these, librarians have become—in addition to being managers of print and electronic materials—business managers.

The new skills required of the contemporary law librarian must include basic accounting skills and the ability to use a spreadsheet. In our library, we analyze each item purchased—how much we pay to purchase it, how much we pay to maintain it, and what the usage is. In addition, we manage desk copies such as court rules so that when attorneys depart the firm, we may retrieve their desk copies for use by new hires. While desk copies are relatively inexpensive, when you are purchasing a lot of them, the cost becomes significant. We analyze online search activity, so that we may offer training to attorneys or paralegals who are using significant amounts of online resources.

For these reasons, I think newer librarians should possess a basic understanding of financial matters. They need to know how to run their library like a business within their firm. The librarian must be a good steward of the firm's resources. If you are going into a special library within a corporation or a law firm, you also need to understand the way that business runs financially, and have a general idea of where expenses are.

The law librarian tries to anticipate attorney needs, which means keeping up with what is new in the legal publishing world. While there is no way to stay abreast of everything new online, one must attempt to catch new developments and services relevant to your firm's practice areas. I rely on the Virtual Chase, the Law Librarian's Research Exchange, beSpacific, Legal Information Alert, and Business Information Alert. I also read the monthly magazines from the American Association of Law Libraries and the Special Libraries Association to keep aware of new publications and services.

One issue that has become increasingly important to the librarian is copyright. It is crucial to maintain awareness of the use of electronic sources. Our firm maintains a strict compliance policy. When I train people entering the firm, it is policy that I tell them flat out: no cover-to-cover copying of print materials and take care that the photocopying falls within fair use. One must be especially judicious in your usage of electronic materials.

The librarian has necessarily become a police officer in this area, because copyright infringement can happen so easily with electronic media. It is critical to monitor your electronic sources closely. This means maintaining lists of who is licensed to use materials, monitoring who is using them, tracking how many licenses you have, and the terms of license agreements. We have found this is best maintained by building a database with all relevant information.

Marketing the Law Library

My firm offers what we call a "coffee break class," which is a ten-minute education session wherein you learn one new concept or technique about the library. The class usually highlights a Web site, but sometimes we highlight print materials as well. A friend who is a librarian in Alabama shared this idea with me, and it is an excellent way to promote the law library internally, within the firm.

To market ourselves internally, we also have a library brochure that we present to new attorneys coming into the firm. This explains services offered by the library, such as news alerts and case tracking. It is a good idea to constantly assert the presence of the library and librarians to attorneys. Essentially, this means saying here we are, and we are ready to help. The physical location of the library can pose a problem with this, in that many libraries are no longer closely tied to the physical space near lawyers' offices. In addition, as electronic sources have expanded and e-mail has become an accepted mode of communication there are not as many people working in the library proper.

With the decrease of foot traffic in the library, lawyers will frequently call or e-mail the library with a question. Often, when you ask whether they have checked a certain set of appropriate books, it seems they have forgotten such print materials exist. This is particularly true with new lawyers, because in law school they are taught via case law, not via topical material. At my firm, we have had new associates who are to be practicing in the intellectual property areas who have never heard of Milgrim on Copyright or Chism on Patents—and those are the seminal treatises for that practice area! A good librarian will steer these people back to the right books, the books they need to do their jobs well. By introducing a variety of materials—print or electronic—librarians can demonstrate how valuable their services are.

Our firm's library presents large-scale promotions of the library twice a year, which include brochures highlighting new items or an ongoing service that has been improved. We also post a "site of the week" on our intranet. Much of what we do for internal marketing is intended to drive people to our intranet page, where users are presented with a wide array of available resources and services—again highlighting the value of the library staff.

Helping Attorneys Help Clients

It is the librarian's duty to provide attorneys with high quality information in a timely fashion, and for as little cost as possible. Keeping your work product high quality, timely, and cost effective is of the essence for lawyers, but more importantly for their clients. I frequently tell lawyers, when I am asked to retrieve something for them, "Good, fast, cheap—pick two." Combining all three qualities in one product is extremely rare. Providing the best quality information in the shortest period of time, and for the least amount of money, supports the goal of making the attorneys well prepared and informed for their clients; this is our supportive function.

While the responsibility of the librarian has expanded primarily in the area of records management and conflicts, the most recent development has been the expansion of librarian responsibility for marketing research and competitive intelligence. In some firms, I have seen this turn into a turf war over who gets to provide the information to the lawyers.

Quite often a librarian will do the necessary background research, cull through materials, prepare the underpinnings of the information, and provide the results to the marketing department, where they then massage the information and do even more sifting. Since lawyers see only the result of all this, they may not perceive what efforts go into it. You need to find ways to make them aware of the part the library plays in the marketing process. In my experience, librarians are highly service oriented, and generally do not actively seek to claim credit for their actions. That appears to me to be the nature of people that go into librarianship, which sometimes is to our detriment, because we shy away from advertising the work we do, or claiming credit where we deserve it.

Within our firm, the library is given credit on the cover page of marketing materials when they are presented to attorneys. By recognizing the library contribution on the front, the marketing department acknowledges the value of our services. It also allows attorneys to contact the researcher, should there be questions on the underlying materials.

Utilizing New Technologies

The trajectory of the law librarian has changed recently due to the explosion of available online materials. This means that librarians have to adapt in new ways. A librarian might be required to fill the role of litigation support expert, or be asked to provide an overview of new software and train new users on it. The librarian is becoming troubleshooter in these and other new areas.

When evaluating new programs and technology, I first look to see if the content offered parallels content we already own. If I am replacing a print set with an electronic set, I look to see if it covers the same period with the same depth of information. The most important consideration is whether the attorney will be able to make use of the new content. When considering a new source, I always ask if it will be user friendly. Most attorneys are either Lexis or Westlaw users, and they use only one service and not the other. You want to avoid the need to train attorneys on a new service unless the content is so valuable to them that they are self-motivated to devote the time and energy it takes.

When an attorney does express interest in learning how to operate a new system, it is essential for the program to be easy to use, and that your instructions are clean and simple. Since most attorneys use only Westlaw and Lexis, it is rare for them to view another service as something they need to learn. Thus, these services (e.g., e-filing) are usually delegated to either the library staff or their assistants, who have adequate time and training for the task.

It is impossible to "prepare" for new developments in technology. Who knew, all those years ago, that something called the Internet was on its way? Yet while it is impossible to prepare for the unknown, it is absolutely fundamental to cultivate adaptability so that when something new does present itself, you are ready to adopt it. This begins with estimating the potential usefulness of a new technology. When faced with a new development, I ask myself how likely it is attorneys will want or need the service. If I decide to go ahead with the service, I make it as easy as possible for them to use. For this to happen, of course, I have to learn it myself, inside and out, so that I have the ability to train others.

Despite the recent shift to electronic resources and data management, there are still things—for example, desk copies of court rules—that attorneys, whether they are young or old, will always want in hard copy form. It may be many years before books disappear altogether, but for the time being we are seeing more dollars move slowly from the print budget over to the electronic budget. As more print sources become available in electronic form, there will be a period of time wherein it will be necessary for librarians to maintain both formats at the same time. It takes a long time to move a person who is accustomed to a print product over to electronic product—unless, of course, the electronic product is extremely easy to use and the content wins the lawyers who want to use it.

In multi-generational law firms, older lawyers generally possess a stronger understanding of the value of print sources. Print sources, in fact, do have advantages in certain areas over their electronic counterparts. For example, when using a print source it is common to stumble across topics in the table of contents or index that are relevant or related to your area of research, but that are worded in differently from your original concept. Thus, a print product can expose a librarian or lawyer to fresh ideas and sources, whereas this ability to browse is rarely accomplished with an electronic product.

Older attorneys also generally have a very thorough understanding of West's Key Number system, which is an enormously helpful legal tool. New attorneys coming straight out of law school usually have never heard of it, and do not know how to use it. This is unfortunate because it is such a valuable tool. On the other hand, younger attorneys are commonly well versed in many of the electronic sources that the older attorneys are not willing to use, or do not understand. It is rare, I think, for a lawyer to be knowledgeable with print sources and technologically savvy. This is indeed unfortunate, because both mediums are useful in their own distinctive ways.

I do think, however, that it is possible for older attorneys to learn to manipulate new technologies. I once had an older partner who realized, because of his grandchildren, that he needed to know how to use the Internet. We sat down together one day, I showed him a few different techniques, and we practiced Web searching together. He eventually became one of the biggest advocates of the Internet and electronic sources.

Another area of change: in the past, law librarians actively facilitated current awareness of various clients and topics; they would read the newspaper each morning, cull through information, and send any relevant articles to various attorneys in their areas of interest. Now that librarians can accomplish this electronically, there has been an explosion of requests for this service. In the past, I followed about ten topics by the old method of scanning the newspaper. Now I have at least a hundred new topical sources that I sort through on behalf of attorneys.

In the area of corporate law, electronic versions of securities filings have made them valuable sources of company information. In the past, when filings were available only in hard copy, they were not quite the same caliber of information source they are today. In the area of intellectual property law, in the past we had to send retrieval services to the Patent and Trademark office to do searches. Those same searches are now available on my desktop. Litigation has also changed because of e-filing, the usefulness of the federal docketing system, and the availability of docket materials, complaints, and materials of this nature. These electronic developments have been a great boon for us.

One source of information that must never be forgotten is, of course, professional colleagues. With the costs of printed materials increasing, librarians certainly cannot afford to own everything we would like to have in our collections. This is why the resource sharing that goes on among librarians is invaluable. Law librarians are always willing to help each other out, and always willing to give their thoughts on how to find a desired source. The Internet has certainly aided communication here as well, in terms of connecting with people looking for similar materials, or who have searched for such things in the past. I find it particularly useful to talk with librarians from corporations because they have a different collection area from my own. For example, a librarian at a food company may have an in-depth understanding of FDA material. It is great to have connections with librarians in the business community, as well as the legal field.

The American Association of Law Libraries (AALL) is a great organization through which one can meet other librarians. The Special Libraries Association (SLA) is a similarly helpful organization. I attend the annual SLA conference more frequently than the Law Librarians Conference since our work has evolved more into business searching and business information. The librarians and vendors at the SLA annual conference have a focus on a wide range of topics, other than legal. I have met librarians who work in museums, Fortune 500 companies, foundations, and think-tanks. Vendors at the SLA conference include online services for company and government information, foreign materials, and industry specific publications. It is an opportunity to expand one's experience beyond the legal field, and get to know sources that may help with our client's information needs.

Conclusion

In responding to the tremendous changes facing the profession of the law librarian, it is essential to cultivate flexibility and always be open to learning new things. It is an effort not to immediately refuse a new service or technology due to cost or the perceived difficulty in making it part of your information offerings. Step back for two minutes and make an effort to understand the possibilities that may be offered. It might turn out to be an opportunity that on the surface looks unappealing. But with time you may see a useful nugget hidden somewhere within it. Be flexible, be open to everybody, and be welcoming to change. Law librarianship today is a changing and challenging area—but it is still a great job.

Cindy Adams attended the University of Florida and received a Bachelor's degree in journalism. While in undergraduate school, she worked in the law school library for Pam Williams, Suzy Gilman Potter and the wonderful Betty Taylor. Because of their example, she decided to attend graduate school in librarianship. Since receiving her Master's degree in librarianship from Emory University, she has worked in several corporate and law firm libraries. Ms. Adams has been with McKenna Long & Aldridge since 1990.